Shakespeare Sonnets as Scenes

The Sonnet as a Storytelling Device

Diane Disque Kurz

Shakespeare Sonnets As Scenes, The Sonnet as a Storytelling Device is a comprehensive guide that empowers beginners and experienced individuals alike to creatively transform sonnets into captivating performances.

Copyright © 2024 Diane Disque Kurz

All rights reserved. No part of this publication may be reproduced or transmitted in any form or by any means, electronic or mechanical, including photocopy, recording, or any information storage and retrieval system, without permission in writing from the publisher.

Printed in the United States.

Cover and book design by Asya Blue Design.

ISBN 979-8-9901164-5-0 Paperback

ISBN 979-8-9901164-4-3 Casebound

Source Material:
William Shakespeare THE SONNETS Poems of Love
St. Martin's Press New York
Copyright © 1980

*To my beloved son, Kelsey,
whose love of Shakespeare, from youth to adulthood,
has inspired me to author this book.*

*And to everyone at any age
who seeks to understand and enjoy William Shakespeare's sonnets.*

*And finally, to William Shakespeare,
without whose genius this book would never be possible.*

Contents

Introduction 1

Chapter One: How Sonnets As Scenes Began 3

Chapter Two: What Are Sonnets as Scenes? 7

Chapter Three: How to Develop a Sonnet as a Scene 13

Chapter Four: Analysis of Sonnet 18 as a Sonnet as a Scene 19

Chapter Five: Working with Multiple Sonnets 23

Chapter Six: From Rehearsal to Performance 27

Chapter Seven: Special Note to Teachers 29

Final Words 31

Appendix A: Sonnets As Scenes Mix and Match 33

Appendix B: Performance Script #1 37

Appendix C: Performance Script #2 53

Appendix D: Sonnets Listed with Storylines 67

Appendix E: Sonnets with Subtext 73

Glossary with Sonnets Listed in Numerical Order 119

Acknowledgments 127

Introduction

"The appropriate business of poetry (which, nevertheless, if genuine is as permanent as pure science) her appropriate employment, her privilege and her duty, is to treat of things not as they are, but as they <u>appear</u>; not as they exist in themselves, but as them <u>seem</u> to exist to the senses and to the passions."

—William Wordsworth
Essay, Supplementary to the Preface
Poems (Wordsworth, 1815) Volume 1/Essay

Imagine a world where spoken poetry is not poetry, but a story told through live performance. Look no further than Shakespeare's collection of 154 sonnets. Each sonnet is a gold mine of authentic thoughts, feelings, and lived experiences. Just as Shakespeare's plays can be validly performed in many ways, so can his sonnets. His plays have been set in Renaissance England, ancient Greece, ancient Egypt, the Wild West, World War II, present day New York City, and many more separate locations and time periods. His plays are universal and timeless.

Why not apply this to his sonnets?

The idea of Sonnets As Scenes is to perform a sonnet, not as a poem, but as a mini-play with a beginning, a middle, and an end. This is an entirely new way to engage with Shakespeare. As Julie Congress, Voice and Text Coach at The Public Theater, said in a recent television documentary, "Shakespeare's hard, but Shakespeare's active. Most of what it is, is finding the effort to say something, both physically and creatively linked." That is what this handbook is all about; one sonnet at a time. It explores how to find the stories in the sonnets and how to develop them physically and creatively into performance-level pieces.

Sonnets As Scenes introduces newcomers to Shakespearean language in a fun, easy fashion. For seasoned actors, Sonnets As Scenes presents a challenge to think outside their classical training. Individuals looking for a good audition piece can work up a sonnet as a scene for their next monologue audition. In classrooms, students exploring Sonnets As Scenes can call upon their creativity and stretch their acting muscles without lengthy rehearsal time. High schools, summer theaters, or community theaters, wanting to explore Shakespeare but not of a mind to produce an entire play, can do an evening of Sonnets As Scenes. After all, a 14-line sonnet takes an average of two minutes to perform making sonnets much easier to stage than an entire Shakespeare production!

Chapter One tells the birth of the Sonnets As Scenes as a concept, then explains the definition of a sonnet in Chapter Two. Chapter Three describes how a sonnet can transform from a poem to a story informed by key words or phrases. A sample analysis of Sonnet 18 breaks down each line with detailed rehearsal and performance advice in Chapter Four. After working with one sonnet and its story, Chapter Five explores how to combine two or more sonnets into mini-plays.

Chapter Six offers suggestions for taking the sonnets from rehearsal spaces to stage. Two Sonnets As Scenes performance scripts are suggested for use as actual performance vehicles in Appendices B and C.

I know firsthand how successful sonnets as scenes can be. My desire is that others will soon know this success. I present this handbook to actors, directors, teachers, students, and lovers of Shakespeare young and old, in the hopes that you find it inspirational, and start on your own sonnets as scenes journey that will be as delightful and rewarding as I have found mine to be.

CHAPTER ONE

How Sonnets As Scenes Began

Growing up, my brother and I had many books, among them a set of young readers that included Shakespeare's stories. My mother read these plain English versions to us, and I fell in love with them. In high school, we studied *Macbeth* and *The Merchant of Venice*. My teacher played a recording on the classroom record player as we followed along in our Penguin paperback books. At first, I did not understand a thing but gradually, phrases started to take on meaning and not only did I fall in love with the story and the characters, but the beautiful language. Years later when I became a parent, I found books like the ones my mother read to me, and I read them to my son, Kelsey. By the time he was ten he was reading them back to me.

Now as adults, Kelsey and I share our love for the Bard. Kelsey is a classically trained actor who loves Shakespeare's play, while I am untrained classically and love his sonnets. The point being that anyone can find something to love about Shakespeare's works.

Completion of this book has taken years. It all began in the summer of 2017 at the New York Renaissance Faire where I was a volunteer and Kelsey was a paid actor and director of the Shakespeare portion of the

3

Faire. This consisted of scenes from Shakespeare's plays. During rehearsals Kelsey gave a sonnet workshop and the half dozen of us who attended memorized sonnets and performed them for the class. I consider my first sonnet, Sonnet 33, "Full many a glorious morning have I seen," a success because I got through it without missing a line.

During that workshop, Kelsey asked our class to take the sonnet we were working on and rewrite it with fewer words while keeping the meanings the same. No one could do it. He told us that the beauty of Shakespeare's sonnets was that there were no wasted words.

That fall, I had multiple surgeries. While recovering I spent hours reading the sonnets. I loved the beauty of the language and how the rhyming patterns were so expertly crafted. I tried to rewrite sonnet after sonnet to no avail. I always needed more words in my rewrites than the sonnet's fourteen lines. Kelsey was right, there were no unnecessary words.

I was hungry to perform another sonnet. Determined to perfect one good enough for the following year's Renaissance Faire, I did a deep dive into Sonnet 18, that everyone knows: "Shall I compare thee to a summer's day?"

The more I read Sonnet 18, the more I saw it in an unusual way, not just as a love poem but as a scene with a beginning, a middle, and an end. It excited me so much that when the next summer came and rehearsals began, I enlisted the help of three young actors, and performed my version of Sonnet 18 as a scene for Kelsey. He loved it! The next thing I knew, we were performing for Renaissance Faire audiences and surprise, surprise – they loved it, too!

"Do you have any more?" I was asked. Well, of course I did. My next entry, Sonnet 75, "So are you to my thoughts as food is to life," is peppered with references to food and eating. Again, this sonnet became a scene, with the character describing something inside a box. I gave it a surprise ending which never ceased to elicit laughter.

The actors asked me if I could find sonnets for them. I wanted the other actors to have as much fun as me, and so did the Renaissance Faire. The next year the Faire permitted me to start a small company of actors to perform the sonnets. I named us *The Sonneteers*. With a stable of sonnets as scenes, we hearty *Sonneteers* embarked on a new adventure.

Honestly, it was difficult. The actors, mostly volunteers, had other Faire duties making rehearsal time short. Even so, we did a variety of sonnets as scenes that year. It seemed that once the actors understood the concept, they could transmit it to the audience. And in turn, the audiences accepted the new concept and reacted enthusiastically. It showed audiences that Shakespeare could be experienced and enjoyed in ways they never expected.

At first, it takes a huge leap of imagination to see a sonnet as a scene. I changed no dialogue. The only requirement was to present the sonnet with a clear story in mind. Once the actors got the hang of thinking freely and experiencing how the stories could come to life, they wholeheartedly bought into the concept, even creating ideas of their own. And thus, sonnets as poems to Sonnets as Scenes was born!

CHAPTER TWO

What Are Sonnets as Scenes?

Simply put, a sonnet is a love poem written to be read. With a few exceptions, it consists of fourteen lines in the rhyming pattern: abab cdcd efef gg. There are three quatrains (sections) of four lines each (abab cdcd efef) with one rhyming couplet, (two lines: gg) at the end. Shakespeare's sonnets are written in iambic pentameter, simply meaning the emphasis on the syllables is short-long, short-long, short-long, short-long, short-long.

Shakespeare wrote 154 sonnets. Many were supposedly written to a "dark lady", possibly a mistress, and were of a sensual nature. Others were supposedly written to a young man with whom, it has been suggested, the poet was in love, even though he urges the young man to marry and have children.

For people well-versed in Shakespearean language, the classical way to perform a sonnet is to recite the sonnet as a poem. Sonnets As Scenes is different in that it is a concept as simple as its name: telling a story by performing a sonnet as a theatrical piece. It is not internal; it is external because it is meant to be viewed by an audience. It can be tricky because Shakespeare was a clever wordsmith who often used puns and riddles in his writing. He was also prone to making up words and, in the article, "Such Ado: The Fight for Shakespeare's Puns" Megan Garber writes, "Shakespeare sounded like all of us, and none of us."

With that quote in mind, I interpret the Bard's words as ambiguous. They frequently have more than one possible meaning, and so I take the liberty of attaching my own meanings to Shakespeare's words when building a scene. I direct the phrases in the sonnets to different individuals or objects instead of one specific lover. The sonnets then become opportunities for actors to stretch their creativity; in this way Shakespeare becomes more understandable and enjoyable.

For example, in Sonnet 75, the first line, "So are you to my thoughts as food is to life," is directed to a box on the actor's lap. At this time, the audience may or may not guess that food is in the box. The sonnet goes on to describe the actor's love of food and his desire to eat it now or wait until later. As the sonnet progresses the actor becomes increasingly agitated with waiting to eat until the end, "Thus do I pine and surfeit day by day, Or gluttoning on all, or all away!" the box is opened and, yes, food, in this case a Ren Faire turkey leg, appears!

Another way to interpret that very same sonnet, Sonnet 75, is with two actors. Imagine a pretty girl watching an egotistical young man eating a piece of pizza. She is talking about the pizza, but the young man thinks she is talking about him. In the end, as she comes close to him, and as he leans forward anticipating her kiss, she snatches his pizza and runs off.

In another example, Sonnet 116, ("Let me not to the marriage of true minds admit impediments, love is not love,") begins with a preacher facing the audience. With her back turned to the audience is a cloaked bride but no groom. On either side are the wedding guests. In comes the bride's father with the reluctant groom. The young man is taken to stand beside the bride. The preacher asks. "If anyone has just cause why this couple should not be wed, speak now or forever hold your peace." Up pops a guest with the first four lines of the sonnet. He thinks he is giving his blessing and stops for applause. The preacher begins again, "If anyone has just cause…" when

WHAT ARE SONNETS AS SCENES?

the same man pops up again because he has more to say. He drones on and on and on as everyone becomes increasingly impatient until we hear a yell from the bride. She is revealed to be pregnant and is now going into labor. The man shouts the last two lines of the sonnet as the bride is carried away by the groom and her father, presumably with the birth of a baby imminent.

My favorite is Sonnet 18, as referenced in the Introduction. The scene opens with a lady sitting on a bench. Beside her, on his knee, with a rose, is a suitor. The lady is flattering him with the first two lines. "Shall I compare thee to a summer's day? Thou art more lovely and more temperate." In the next two lines she has doubts that he is the right one; "Rough winds do shake the darling buds of May, and summer's lease hath all too short a date." At this time, another suitor with a rose enters and goes down on one knee on the other side of the lady. The second four lines she directs to him in the same manner as she did to suitor number one. The first two lines are her positively considering him and the second two lines she again becomes doubtful. Back and forth this goes until the last two lines when the lady stands agonizing over which suitor her heart will choose; "So long as men can breathe or eyes can see *(who do I choose?)* So long lives this, and this gives life…"*(my heart)* when she sees a third man cross the stage in front of her - "to thee!" And off she goes with him.

Each of these examples is as much fun for the actors as they are for the audience.

Each requires only one person to memorize a sonnet, though they may require more actors. Sonnet 75 (turkey leg or pizza) can be performed as a solo or with two people. Sonnet 18 (two suitors) needs four people and Sonnet 116 (shotgun wedding) is an ensemble piece.

I usually get my sonnet story ideas from the words and phrases of the sonnet I am reading. As I write this, Sonnet 141 comes to mind; "In faith I do not love thee with mine eyes." A story pops into my mind about a pair of robots trying to express their love to each other in very mechanical terms. What fun this could be to stage! Remember, what the famous intellectual historian, Mary Carruthers, reminds us, "People do not have ideas; they make them."

Without going into detail, some other sonnets that shout their storylines to me are:

Sonnet 26   ("Lord of my love, to whom in vassalage.")
Girl trying to give a love note to a soldier at attention

Sonnet 41   ("Those pretty wrongs that liberty commits.")
Boyfriend spying on his girlfriend, thinking she is cheating on him

Sonnet 53   ("What is your substance, whereof are you made?")
Girl dreams of a fairy friend who appears before her

Sonnet 57   ("Being your slave, what should I do but tend.")
Fool to his Queen

Sonnet 66   ("Tir'd with all these, for restful death I cry.")
General and his troops surviving a losing battle

Sonnet 74   ("But be contented. When that fell arrest.")
Possible Curtain Call with multiple actors trading lines

Sonnet 109   ("O, never say that I was false of heart.")
Man, as his dog lays dying

Sonnet 128   ("How oft, when thou, my music, music play'st.")
Girl groupie tells her love for a musician to his instrument

Sonnet 130   ("My mistress' eyes are nothing like the sun.")
Man complimenting his lady in awkward fashion

Sonnet 138   ("When my love swears that he is made of truth")
Older woman (cougar) about her young lover

Sonnet 139   ("O, call not me to justify the wrong.")
Man dying in battle with his trusty sword

WHAT ARE SONNETS AS SCENES?

Sonnet 145   ("Those lips that Love's own hand did make.")
                   A mother trying to communicate with her daughter who refuses to answer until the last line.

As you can see, a sonnet as scene is simply a sonnet telling a story. The more you do the easier they become. All it takes is total commitment to the story being told.

Appendix D provides a complete list of sonnets with brief storylines that we *Sonneteers* worked on, some to performance level, others just for fun.

It is important to note that at any time there is a gender referenced in this book, it is only a suggestion. The beauty of the sonnets as scenes is they are gender neutral. The roles can be assigned as the actors and directors see fit, or as the number of participants allows.

CHAPTER THREE

How to Develop a Sonnet as a Scene

To develop a sonnet as a scene, find a sonnet that speaks to you. Read it aloud a few times. First read the sonnet for the rhyming and make a note of any major idea that pops into your head. Next read it for key words that support that idea. Don't worry if it doesn't make sense at this point. All you're doing is letting the words and/or phrases inspire you. From there you can develop a story to tell.

The famous 13th century poet, Rumi, wrote:

"Listen to *presences* inside poems.

Let them take you where they will.

Follow those private hints,

And never leave the *premises.*"

In other words, the clues (presences) to the story are in the poem (sonnet) and they will guide you within the premises (the story you are telling.)

For example, Sonnet 75 talks about food. "So are you to my thoughts as food is to life!" What story can be told around food? The sonnet builds at a "hungry" pace. Why not have it about food instead of a person?

Another example is Sonnet 43 that begins, "When most I wink, then do mine eyes best see…" The scene starts with seeing then passes into sleep, "But when I sleep, in dreams they look on thee." Since the Renaissance Faire had fairies, we used a fairy to wake up a sleeping man. During the sonnet he tries to connect with her and she with him, but a thin unseen veil keeps them apart. He closes the sonnet realizing that he cannot have her awake and she knowing this also, puts him back to sleep. "All days are nights to see till I see thee, and nights bright days when dreams do show thee me." Dream and sleep were the key words inspiring this story.

Sonnet 144 is a scene with four actors. Picture a guy finding a purse with money in it. Then we see a girl come looking for it as he hides it away from her. Not finding her purse, she goes off crying. The guy has a choice to make - does he give her back the purse or keep it? Now appear his two spirits; one good, one evil. "Two loves I have of comfort and despair, which like two spirits do suggest me still." As he recites the sonnet the dueling spirits try to convince him of their sides. In the end, "Yet this shall I ne'er know, but live in doubt, till my bad angel fire my good one out." He then keeps the purse. Or, the actors can decide he gives it back. It works either way. The key words, good and evil, however, are what began the creative process that led to this story.

Pay attention to punctuation. It will help you determine where to take pauses, where to emphasis certain sections, or even where to take breaths. A semicolon will many times indicate a break in thought from one thought to another completely different thought. Also, notice that some of the words at the end of the sentences don't always rhyme in the way that we pronounce them nowadays, so you may choose to change the pronunciations to make them rhyme. For example, in Sonnet 29's second quatrain it says:

HOW TO DEVELOP A SONNET AS A SCENE

> "Wishing me like to one more rich in hope,
>
> Featured like him, like him with friends *possessed*,
>
> Desiring this man's art, and that man's scope,
>
> With what I most enjoy contented *least*."

In Shakespeare's day, the words "possessed" and "least" may have rhymed. In our day they do not. Some actors choose to pronounce the words correctly. I choose to change the words so they rhyme. "Least" becomes "lest" and now they rhyme. The meaning doesn't change only the pronunciation. The audience will understand the meaning. Simply, enjoy the words and the rhymes as they fall off the tongue. Sonnets ("little songs") are, after all, musical. Use their "music" to focus on how the sonnet sounds.

Some sonnets have repeated words that give clues to a possible theme for a storyline. For example, Sonnet 75 talks about "food" which literally became about food.

Many sonnets have lists of things the poet uses to make his point. These lists are wonderful fodder for creatively interpreting the story's theme. For example, Sonnet 19 has an extensive list before the story reveals the reason for it:

> "Devouring Time, 1) blunt thou the lion's paws,
>
> And make the earth devour her own sweet brood;
>
> 2) Pluck the keen teeth from the fierce tiger's jaws,
>
> And burn the long-lived phoenix in her blood;
>
> 3) Make glad and sorry seasons as thou fleets,
>
> And do whate'er thou wilt, swift-footed Time,
>
> To the wide world and all her fading sweets;"

Those were the lists that lead up to what the sonnet is really about:

"But I forbid thee one most heinous crime,

O, carve not with thy hours my love's fair brow,

Nor draw no line there with thine antique pen."

Imagine a hospital waiting room, where a man is waiting to hear if his loved one will survive. He is bargaining with Time (or maybe God, the Grimm Reaper, etc.?) In the end, a doctor comes out and simply shakes his head, indicating, what the man did not want, death.

Not all lines and/or phrases make perfect sense. There may be a sonnet that you read and reread that speaks to you in one specific way. Or as many times as you reread a particular sonnet, you find as many different meanings. Not every sonnet that tells a story will be easy to stage. This is where the actor guides the words and phrases to mean what the story requires them to mean. It takes a total commitment to the story being told rather than to the poem itself. Shakespeare played with words and phrases, making some up, using them in unique ways, particularly puns. Why not use those same words and give them innovative meanings? Look up words in the dictionary to see what they mean. That may help in deciding if you will keep that meaning or make up a new one. You can also use the Glossary at the end of this book.

After analyzing your sonnet, you may find the idea doesn't translate as clearly as you saw it in your mind. Is it because it is too difficult or have you not committed to it entirely? The only way to answer that question is to jump in and try it out.

I caution you not to give up too soon. When presenting a sonnet clear choices are best. Have someone watch the scene, then ask them: Did it make sense? Why or why not? Did you stop listening? Why or why not? This will help you find the spots to give a little more attention to.

The key is to totally memorize the sonnet. Many words and phrases are tongue twisters and only through repetition will they flow as needed for the scene. When memorizing always think of the story you are telling, allowing you to emphasize the words that support the story. Stay true to the story and use the words and actions that support it.

Use the first rehearsal to read the sonnet and determine how the scene will flow and what your words mean to the storyline. Then, during blocking (where the actors on stage determine where to stand) add the non-speaking actors. But be creative! Many times, those non-speaking actors prove to be essential in adding details and meaning to the scene. They are also important in establishing the rhythm of the sonnet. Is it comical? Does the pace need to move quickly, urgently? Is it dramatic? Do the actors need to take their time? Is there a set-up before the sonnet begins? What props will provide context for the story? All this, and more, can be provided by the non-speaking actors.

The rehearsal period can be very enjoyable if the actors let their creativity guide them. Many times, we, *Sonneteers*, ended up laughing and taking the sonnet to the extreme only to see that what we thought was outrageous was the best way to tell the story.

One outrageous example is Sonnet 68, ("Thus is his cheek the map of days outworn.") I originally saw it as two gravediggers at the site of the grave before the corpse was put in. They knew the deceased and were trading lines back and forth lamenting his passing. The actors would take sips from the dead man's flask. During rehearsals, the actors began checking the dead man's pockets as they said their lines stealing the dead man's flask, watch, scarf, boots, and hat. The best part was after all of that, the dead man wakes up and snatches back his flask. Whereupon the two gravediggers run away in fright. The dead man then takes a swig from his flask and passes out. It was outrageous and hilarious. The actors were able to take this sonnet to the next level because they knew their lines completely and thoroughly and were able to match the pacing of the story with the language.

I said it before but it bears repeating: the most important advice I can give you for rehearsal success is to learn the lines. Totally learn the sonnet.

The most important note I can give you for performance success is always support the main actor(s) delivering the line(s) by giving them the focus! Because we are asking the audience to accept our version of what the words mean, they need to clearly hear the words and understand what the actor is trying to say. If the focus is elsewhere, you risk losing the audience's attention. This destroys the story's momentum you have been building. Remember, a sonnet takes only a few minutes to perform. Every second counts. Once you lose the audience you seldom get them back because there simply isn't enough time.

Use the examples that are provided in Appendix A to workshop the different stories. Or, pick others from the 154 sonnets available. There is endless material to work with!

CHAPTER FOUR

Analysis of Sonnet 18 as a Sonnet as a Scene

Shakespeare writes his sonnets in an Act 1, Act 2, Act 3 sort of way. Generally, he uses the first two quatrains, lines 1-8, to introduce the initial point of the sonnet (Act 1) the next quatrain, lines 9-12, to present a counterargument to the initial point (Act 2), and the final lines, the couplet, to summarize the poem, drawing its conclusion (Act 3.)

With this in mind, this chapter fully examines Sonnet 18. This sample sonnet is meant to provide the actor with the tools to break down the sonnet's "Acts" and use subtext to tell the story. What helps the actor tell a clear story is the subtext – found in every line – which reveals the thoughts and motivations behind the spoken words. Stay true to the subtext and the story tells itself. By playing to (or acting) the subtext, the words fall into place.

Sonnet 18 begins with a lady sitting on a bench. Next to her is Suitor One down on one knee. He is handing her a rose. She looks at him favorably as she says the first two lines; "Shall I compare thee to a summer's day? Thou art more lovely and more temperate."

She then thinks a beat. Perhaps he is too young for her. Looking forward, away from him, she says the next two lines, "Rough winds do shake the darling buds of May, and summer's lease hath all too short a date."

Suitor Two now enters and kneels on her other side, offering a rose. She takes one look at him and is immediately attracted to him. Her next lines are to him. "Sometimes too hot the eye of heaven shines and often is his gold complexion dimmed." To her, this suitor is "hot" – even sexier than the sun!

Again, she takes a beat to think this through. Is this man going to have the stamina to keep up with me? Facing forward she says, "And every fair from fair sometime declines, by chance or by nature's changing course, untrimmed."

Two suitors are now vying for her affection. The next lines are her going back and forth between the two men trying to decide which one to pick. To Suitor One she says, "But thy eternal summer shall not fade, nor lose possession of the fair thou oust." Oh, I'm sure he will be wonderful! Back to Suitor Two; "Nor shall death brag thou, wonder'rest in its shade, when in eternal lines to Time thou grow'st." Maybe, just maybe he can keep up with me. Hmmm.

Knowing she has to decide; she ponders one last time between the two. To herself more than to the gentlemen, she becomes determined to choose with her heart. "So long as men can live or eyes can see, so long lives this," (motioning to her heart.) "And this gives life…" Right then a third man walks across the stage and catches her eye. At that moment, her choice is the third man, "to thee!" She walks off with him to the dismay of the two suitors who are left only with roses.

Using the Act 1, Act 2, Act 3 approach, we see lines 1-8 are the setup, lines 9-12, are the problem to be solved, and, lines 13-14, the conclusion. Once the acts are put together, you have a sonnet as a scene. One act flows into the next and in two to three minutes a new creation exists!

This sonnet is only for example purposes. You may choose to go in an entirely different direction. That is what makes sonnets as scenes so much fun. The possibilities are endless.

ANALYSIS OF SONNET 18 AS A SONNET AS A SCENE

Note: This sonnet does not have to be done with a girl and three male suitors. It can be adapted to any and/or all genders.

SONNET 18
"Shall I compare thee to a summer's day?"

LADY FAIR:	SUBTEXT

(Sitting on bench, to Suitor One kneeling to her right)

Shall I compare thee to a summer's day?	Ah yes, thou art fine indeed.
Thou art more lovely and more temperate.	
Rough winds do shake the darling buds of May,	But maybe you are too young for me.
And summer's lease hath all too short a date.	

(To Suitor Two, who has entered and kneels to her left)

Sometime too hot the eye of heaven shines,	My goodness, how sexy!
And often is his gold complexion dimmed;	
And every fair from fair sometime declines,	But your older age may not keep up!
By chance, or nature's changing course, untrimmed	

(Back to Suitor One)

| But thy eternal summer shall not fade, | Maybe I spoke too soon. |
| Nor lose possession of that fair thou ow'st, | |

(Back to Suitor Two)

| Nor shall death brag thou wand'rest in his shade, | Then again, you might keep up. |
| When in eternal lines to Time thou grow'st. | |

(Stands, trying to make up her mind between the two)

| So long as men can breathe, or eyes can see, | Oh dear, who to choose? |
| So long lives this, and this gives life to ... | My heart. |

(Handsome man walks across stage and Lady Fair sees him.)

| thee! | I'll give my heart to him! |

(Lady Fair follows Handsome Man leaving two suitors crest fallen.)

CHAPTER FIVE

Working with Multiple Sonnets

Once you have the knack, sonnets can be combined to make miniplays. Below are some ways to combine sonnets to achieve this.

Sonnet 33 and Sonnet 68 make a good combination. The scene would be at a gravesite. As the gravediggers bring in the body, the widow comes to say her final goodbye with Sonnet 33. After she leaves the gravediggers do their Sonnet 68 (as described in Chapter Three) lamenting the death of their friend and are startled when the "dead" friend wakes up from his drunken stupor.

Another good combination is Sonnet 14 and Sonnet 116. It begins with three witches reciting the first well known scene from Macbeth. ("When shall we three meet again?") They approach the girl wrapped in a cloak with Sonnet 14 and its predictions. ("Not from the stars do I my judgment pluck.") As the wedding guests approach, the witches leave and in comes the bride's father with the reluctant groom and all the wedding guests. The preacher begins with, "We are gathered here today… If anyone can show just cause why this couple should not be lawfully wed…" At this point one guest launches into Sonnet 116 with; "Let me not to the marriage of true minds…" Throughout the rest of the scene this guest keeps interjecting so that the preacher never gets to the actual "I dos." Right

SHAKESPEARE SONNETS AS SCENES

before the final couplet the bride cries out and we realize she is pregnant and going into labor. The father and groom carry her out as the gutsy guest yells the final lines to them.

Consider sonnets, 18, 141, 147, and 120, in that order. After the girl has left with the third man in Sonnet 18, the two remaining suitors stay and, exchanging quatrains from each of their sonnets (Suitor One does Sonnet 141; Suitor Two does Sonnet 147), they lament losing the girl. (See Appendix F for the two sonnets combined.) They exchange drinks from a flask. Sonnet 120 begins when the girl and her new beau (third man in Sonnet 18) come back arguing. She feels he has wronged her, while he feels she is being hard on him. They go back and forth being angry, until their anger reaches a fever pitch, whereupon they decide they want each other badly. The suitors watch all of this and are rooting for the girl to give the guy the heave-ho. But, alas, in the end, the couple go off very much in love while the suitors pass the flask one more time.

Another good matchup is sonnets 69, 3, and 62 in that order. This mini-play is about a man who does not respond to a girl picked out for him by his mother. Sonnet 69 is the girl attempting to get his attention to no avail. Sonnet 3 is his mother nagging him to which he ignores her. As a passing artist suggests she can draw a picture of the man and his girlfriend, the man, heartily agrees. He goes into Sonnet 62, holding a mirror to his egotistical face, as the artist sketches on her drawing board. In the end, the artist produces a masterpiece of his girlfriend and a donkey's ass. The man is appalled but the girl and his mother find this hilarious.

Interlacing the actions of different sonnets can be tricky but so much fun. Even though each of these sonnets can stand alone, Sonnet 148 and Sonnet 50, respectively, is one of these tricky combinations. Picture a boy and girl. The girl snatches the near-sighted boyfriend's glasses from his face. She teases him to come and find her. He begins Sonnet 148, ("O me! What eyes hath love put in my head, which have no correspondence with true sight!") She continues to tease him with his glasses as he says, "Or - if they have, where is my judgment fled, that censures falsely what they see aright?" At this point a couple who have obviously traveled a long way and still have a long way to go, enter. She is so weary that he decides to carry her with Sonnet 50. "How heavy do I journey on the way when what I seek my weary travel's end. Doth teach that ease and that repose to say, thus far the miles are measured from thy friend." She gets on him piggy back style and off they go. The first couple continue their game of "come find me" with the next lines, "If that be fair whereon my false eyes do dote, what means the world to say it is not so? If it be not, then love doth well denote love's eye is not so true as all men's 'no.'"

Back comes the second couple with the girl still on his back, obviously tired and lost. He continues, "The beast that bears me, tired with my woe, plods (dully) on, to bear that weight in me. As if by some instinct that wretch did know his rider lov'd not speed, being made from thee." During the speech, the girl kicks him to go faster as if he were a horse, only concerned about her own comfort. He is not too happy about this but keeps on going and they exit. Now the first couple comes alive again, the boy in this couple increasingly frustrated. "O how can love's eye be true, that is so vexed with watching and with tears? No marvel then, though I mistake my view; The sun itself see not til heaven clears."

And guess what? The first couple comes back. The man is plodding along; "The bloody spur cannot provoke him on, that sometimes anger thrusts into his hide, which heavily he answers with a groan, more sharp to me than spurring to his side." During this his partner does everything she can to make him go faster, but he has had enough and now delivers the last two lines as he drops her on the floor; "For that same groan doth put this in my mind: my grief lies onward and my joy behind." He storms off leaving her on the ground.

The first couple are now separated by this bewildered second girl. As the first man reaches for his glasses, he falls over the second woman on the ground.

The two make instant contact and he quickly decides that this one may be better than the first one as he says to his now former girlfriend;

"With tears thou keep'st me blind, lest eyes well selling thy foul faults should find." He helps the second woman onto his back as she gives him directions on which way to go, leaving the first girl with only a pair of glasses. For a different ending see Sonnet 50/Sonnet 148 right after Sonnet 50 in Appendix E.

Timing is everything in the mini-play. It needs to move seamlessly from one sonnet to the next to work. It also involves much physical activity between the partners, so blocking smoothly is essential. The mini-play is challenging but not impossible and the rewards are immense!

Originally, we had Sonnet 50 be between a guard and his prisoner on their way to the prison. That worked, too. We didn't use it at the Renaissance Faire because it was too dramatic. We wanted our sonnets to be happy and fun. There may be a way of telling a story with Sonnet 50 that is yet to be discovered. The beauty of all of this is there is no wrong answer!

Also, don't be afraid to change dialogue from one character to another in the sonnets. If the story is best told by giving some of the other characters dialogue, go right ahead!

Appendix A, Sonnets As Scenes Mix and Match, has more sonnets with suggested pairings.

CHAPTER SIX

From Rehearsal to Performance

Knowing how to analyze, explore, and create a sonnet as a scene is the first part in bringing a sonnet as a story to life. The second part is deciding how, when, and where you want to perform it.

As part of an acting class, scene study, or creative play you may decide to do one sonnet at a time with different actors rehearsing their own sonnet and presenting it to the entire class. Or a community theatre, summer theatre, or senior center may want to make an evening of Sonnets as Scenes for the theatre going public. Originally, these were the venues I pictured when I decided to write this handbook. There are many other venues where sonnets as scenes could be done: nursing homes, arts fairs, parks, and, of course, middle-school, high-school, and college classrooms.

Performance Scripts #1 and #2 (Appendices B and C) are included for anyone wanting a ready-made program. Each script is approximately 20-30 minutes long and can be combined for a longer program. Also, included is Sonnets As Scenes Mix and Match in Appendix A. You can go there and pick and choose the sonnets you would like to develop into a performance script of your own.

When working with the sonnets as scenes you may discover more sonnets as scenes than the thirty, I referenced here. I urge you to use your own imagination and construct your own sonnets into mini-plays. Don't be afraid to try any and everything you conceive. You may be surprised - and your future audiences will benefit greatly from this new, unique theatre experience you offer them.

CHAPTER SEVEN

Special Note to Teachers

The conventional wisdom teaching Shakespeare, when I was young and may still be today, was Shakespeare as English Literature. It was read in class and studied as you would a novel or a poem. One result was that many students were completely turned off by Shakespeare and dreaded the time of the school year when they had to read his plays. Sonnets as scenes takes a different approach. By starting with sonnets using storylines to tell a short story, the student has an opportunity to discover Shakespeare in a way that is not frightening or intimidating and can actually be fun.

In the late 1500s, early 1600s, 95% of the audiences at the Olde Globe for a Shakespeare play were illiterate, could not read or write. Shakespeare wrote his plays to be performed, to be seen live. He never meant them to be studied as literature. By using the sonnets as scenes to introduce students to Shakespeare, the students can take a small bite of Shakespeare and get used to him before tackling his larger and more complex plays. The students can feel the words in their mouths and use them to physically tell a story. Remember, Shakespeare's works had close to 2,000 made-up words. The audience at the time didn't know his unfamiliar words or what they meant. With the sonnets as scenes the students can use their creativity and imagination to put meanings to his words to tell a story.

I am not a teacher, nor do I mean to present myself as one. However, I see the value of being taught Shakespeare with sonnets as scenes first. I think students could enjoy them in a way that might peak their interest in his plays when the time comes to study them in high school or college. To see Shakespeare as live and engaging, instead of pages to be read, can't hurt. So, to all you open-minded teachers out there who have picked up this book and are wondering how and if this is something that could be of value to you in your classrooms, please try them. I know there may be English teachers that dread teaching Shakespeare. These sonnets as scenes can help you engage with students and have fun doing it.

Doing Sonnets as Scenes Workshops with high school students has proven to me that this method of teaching Shakespeare works. At the end of one of the workshops, during the question-and-answer session, one of the students said that the previous year she hated Shakespeare when they did it, but the workshop was so much fun she was really looking forward to when they did Shakespeare that year.

It works, and I urge you to give it a try with your students.

Final Words

To those of you who are pondering memorizing sonnets and performing them in storytelling form, I urge you to act and do it! If it seems confusing, it is. But that is where you can use your imagination to clarify a story. Even if you feel as though you are speaking in another language, make the language yours. Understand only what you want to understand and diminish the rest. It works. You can do this and it can be fun. Jump in!

To those of you who gave it a try and had fun doing it, I applaud you. You have done something few have chosen to do; expanded your creativity, undertook the Bard, and found joy and a sense of accomplishment. Keep at it!

To those of you who gave sonnets as scenes a try and believe you have not succeeded; you should know that is not true. You have experienced Shakespearean language in its rawest form, using words and phrases so different from your everyday vocabulary. And now, hopefully, you have a greater respect for what it takes to understand and perform Shakespeare's works. I applaud you, too!

And so, we come to the end of Sonnets As Scenes, The Sonnet as a Storytelling Device. My initial goal in authoring this book was to preserve the concept and examples for others to use when discovering the joys of performing sonnets as stories. I invite you to take this book to a group of like-minded individuals and knock yourselves out breathing life into centuries old sonnets. You don't need to achieve performance level. All you and your group need to do is interpret the traditional form of the Shakespearean sonnet in a distinctive nontraditional way and have fun doing so!

There is an artist named Suzanne Coley who makes embroidered copies of the sonnets on quilts. That is where her imagination took her. There are unique ways to interpret Shakespeare's sonnets that haven't even been thought of yet. You can think of them. The beauty of Sonnets as Scenes is that there is no limit to what you can create and have fun doing so!

Of course, Sonnets As Scenes would not be complete without an ending. Consider Sonnet 74 ("But be contented. When that fell arrest without bail shall carry me away.") It works with one speaker or many speakers sharing lines. We *Sonneteers* found this sonnet difficult to create a specific story around but, as a finale, it can be interpreted to mean saying "goodbye" and so we used it for our curtain call.

I leave you with the couplet from Sonnet 74: "The worth of that is that which it contains, and that is this, and this with thee remains."

THE END

APPENDIX A

Sonnets As Scenes Mix and Match

See Appendix E for all the sonnets with their subtext.

Note. These sonnets can be adapted to any and/or all genders.

ONE PERSON SONNET AS SCENE

Actor may choose a character to express the meaning of the story. For example: the character in Sonnet 33 could be a girl whose boyfriend has broken up with her or a widow who has lost the love of her life.

Sonnet 29	"When, in disgrace with Fortune and men's eyes."
Sonnet 33	"Full many a glorious morning have I seen."
Sonnet 75	"So are you to my thoughts as food to life."
Sonnet 109	"O, never say that I was false of heart."
Sonnet 138	"When my love swears that she is made of truth."
Sonnet 139	"O, call not me to justify the wrong."
Sonnet 141	"In faith I do not love thee with mine eyes."
Sonnet 147	"My love is as a fever, longing still."

TWO PERSONS SONNETS AS SCENES

One speaking role with a supporting nonspeaking role.

Sonnet 14	"Not from the stars do I my judgment pluck."
Sonnet 19	"Devouring Time, blunt thou the lion's paws."

Sonnet 26	"Lord of my love, to whom in vassalage."
Sonnet 33	"Full many a glorious morning have I seen."
Sonnet 43	"When most I wink, then do mine eyes best see."
Sonnet 53	"What is your substance, whereof are you made."
Sonnet 57	"Being your slave, what should I do but tend?"
Sonnet 69	"These parts of thee that the world's eye doth view."
Sonnet 75	"So are you to my thoughts as food to life."
Sonnet 148	"O me, what eyes hath Love put in my head."

TWO PERSONS SONNETS AS SCENES
Two speaking roles

Sonnet 50	"How heavy do I journey on the way."
Sonnet 68	"Thus is his cheek the map of days outworn." (with supporting nonspeaking role)
Sonnet 120	"That you were once unkind befriends me now."
Sonnet 145	"Those lips that Love's own hand did make."
Sonnet 148	"O me, what eyes hath Love put in my head."

THREE OR MORE PERSONS SONNETS AS SCENES
One speaking role with supporting nonspeaking roles

Sonnet 18	"Shall I compare thee to a summer's day."
Sonnet 46	"Mine eye and heart are at a mortal war."
Sonnet 66	"Tired with all these, for restful death I cry."
Sonnet 144	"Two loves I have, of comfort and despair."

THREE OR MORE PERSONS SONNETS AS SCENES
Multiple speaking roles with supporting speaking and nonspeaking roles

Sonnet 14	"Not from the start do I my judgment pluck."
Sonnet 74	"But be contented. When that fell arrest."
Sonnet 116	"Let me not to the marriage of true minds."
Sonnet 128	"How oft, when thou, my music, music play'st."

SONNETS AS SCENES MIX AND MATCH

TWO OR MORE SONNETS AS MINI-PLAYS

Sonnets 69, 3, 62	"Those parts of thee that the world's eye doth view."
	"Look in thy glass and tell the face thou viewest."
	"Those parts of thee that the world's eye doth view."
Sonnets 33, 68	"Many a glorious morning have I seen."
	"Thus is his cheek the map of days outworn."
Sonnets 18, 141/147, 120	"Shall I compare thee to a summer's day."
	"In faith I do not love thee with mine eyes."
	"My love is as a fever, longing still."
	"That you were once unkind befriends me now."
Sonnets 50/148	""How heavy do I journey on the way."
	"O me, what eyes hath Love put in my head."

APPENDIX B

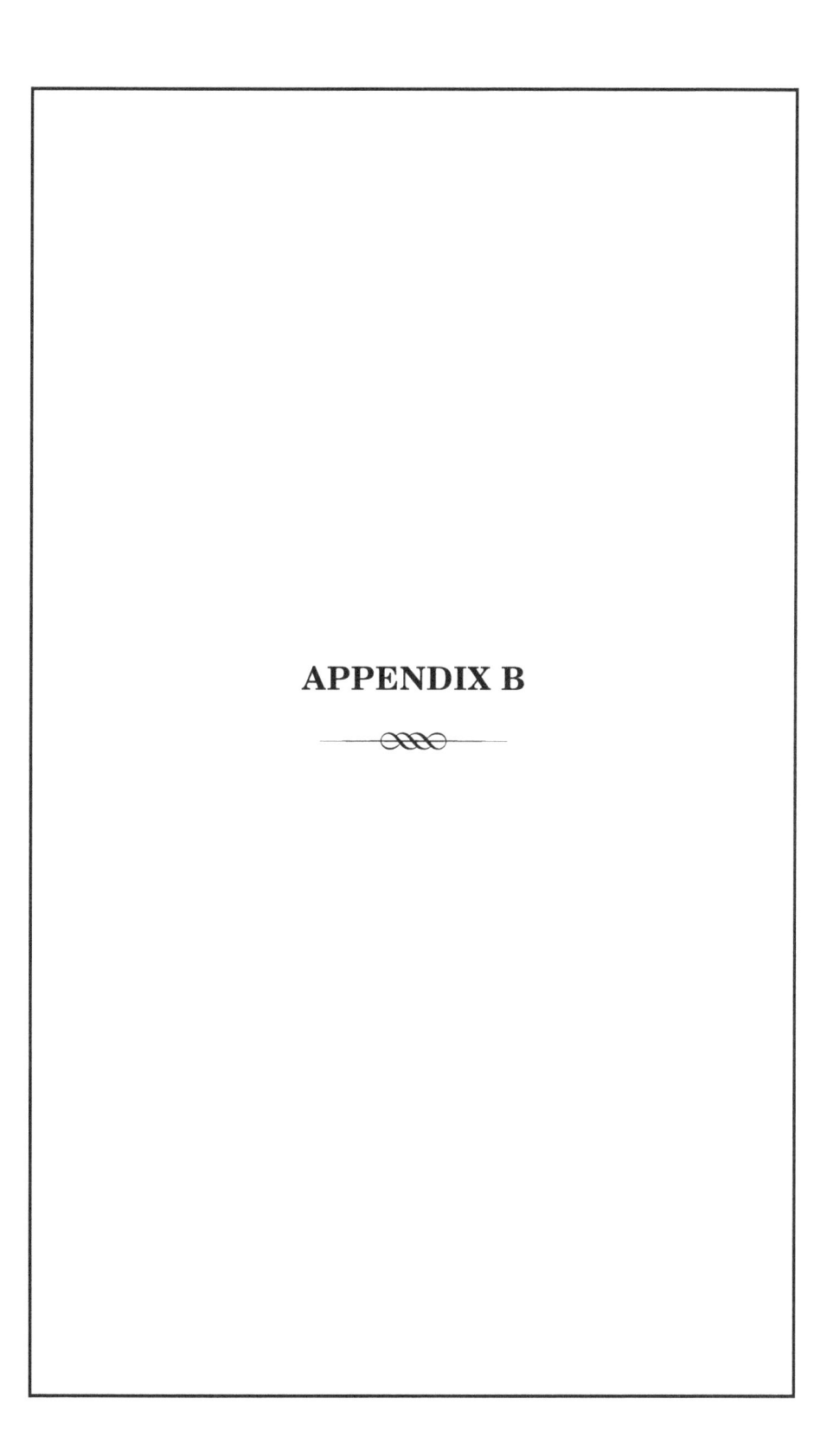

SHAKESPEARE
SONNETS AS SCENES
_____

"Performance Script #1"

SHAKESPEARE SONNETS AS SCENES

"Cast of Characters"

Sonnets: 18, 29, 33, 68, 74, 120, 141, 147

Length: approximately 35 minutes

Suggested Cast: 6-8 actors including Narrator
Parts to be decided between the actors and their director

Props: book of sonnets (Narrator), pen, letters (sonnets 29 and 33), handkerchief (Sonnet 33), hat, scarf, watch, boots, etc.(Sonnet 68), roses (Sonnet 18)

Costumes: limited only by the creativity of the actors

This script can be combined with Performance Script #2 for a longer presentation.

*See Appendix E in *Sonnets As Scenes, The Sonnet as a Story-telling Device*, for each sonnet with its text and subtext.

"PERFORMANCE SCRIPT #1"

NARRATOR

"Look not with the eyes. But with the mind, and therefore, is winged Cupid painted blind." Ah, Shakespeare. He wrote so beautifully.

> (From A Midsummer Night's Dream:
> Act 1/Scene 1. Actor can choose to tell audience source of quote, nor not.)

PERFORMANCE SCRIPT #1

"Shakespeare Sonnets as Scenes." Don't we actors love alliteration? Just what is a Sonnet as a Scene you may ask? The idea is to perform a Shakespeare sonnet, not as a love poem, but as a mini-play with a beginning, a middle, and an end. But first, let us present a sonnet the way it is usually done, as a love poem being recited by a single actor. Most of the words in Shakespeare's sonnets may sound foreign and not of this age, but you will understand them in no time. Let's see…

    (Narrator flips through book he is holding.)

Aah… Sonnet 29 fits the bill.

                 SONNET 29
                    ACTOR
When in disgrace with fortune and men's eyes,
I all alone beweep my outcast state,
And trouble deaf heaven with my bootless cries,
And look upon myself and curse my fate,

Wishing me like to one more rich in hope,
Featured like him like him with friends possessed,
Desiring this man's art and that man's scope,
With what I most enjoy contented least;

Yet in these thoughts myself almost despising,
Haply I think on thee, and then my state,
Like to the lark at break of day arising
From sullen earth, sings hymns at heaven's gate;

For thy sweet love rememb'red such wealth brings,
That then I scorn to change my state with kings.

                    NARRATOR
Let us now present, for you, the same sonnet, Sonnet
29 combined with Sonnet 33, only with a soldier,
at war, writing to his girlfriend back home in the
States.

                    SONNET 29
                    SOLDIER
          (A soldier, on one side of the stage
          reading aloud the letter he is
          writing to his fiancée. His fiancée
          is on the other side of the stage
          reading it silently as he speaks. At
          sonnet's end, the soldier exits.)

When in disgrace with fortune and men's eyes,
I all alone beweep my outcast state,
And trouble deaf heaven with my bootless cries,
And look upon myself and curse my fate,

Wishing me like to one more rich in hope,
Featured like him like him with friends possessed,
Desiring this man's art and that man's scope,
With what I most enjoy contented least;

Yet in these thoughts myself almost despising,
Haply I think on thee, and then my state,
Like to the lark at break of day arising
From sullen earth, sings hymns at heaven's gate;

42

PERFORMANCE SCRIPT #1

For thy sweet love rememb'red such wealth brings,
That then I scorn to change my state with kings.

SONNET 33
SOLDIER'S PARTNER
(The soldier's partner opens another
official looking letter and reads it.
She has just been informed that
her fiancée was killed in action.
Sonnet 33 is her response.)

Full many a glorious morning have I seen
Flatter the mountaintops with sovereign eye,
Kissing with golden face the meadows green;
Gilding pale streams with heavenly alchemy;

Anon permit the basest clouds to ride
With ugly rack on his celestial face,
And from the forlorn world his visage hide,
Stealing unseen to west with this disgrace.

Even so my sun one early morn did shine,
With all triumphant splendor on my brow;
But out alack, he was but one hour mine,
The region cloud hath masked him from me now.

Yet him for this my love no whit disdaineth;
Suns of the world may stain when heaven's sun staineth.

NARRATOR
How tragic. Let's lighten it up a bit, again using one of the same sonnets from above, paired with a

new sonnet. Consider a graveyard. Oh, dear. Looks
like someone has died. We see the dearly departed
and the widow with the gravediggers who happen to be
close friends of the deceased.

>   SONNET 33
>   WIDOW/WIDOWER
>   (During sonnet gravediggers weeping
>   constantly interrupts the widow's
>   sonnet. When the widow finishes
>   talking, she leaves.)

Full many a glorious morning have I seen
Flatter the mountaintops with sovereign eye,
Kissing with golden face the meadows green;
Gilding pale streams with heavenly alchemy;

Anon permit the basest clouds to ride
With ugly rack on his celestial face,
And from the forlorn world his visage hide,
Stealing unseen to west with this disgrace.

Even so my sun one early morn did shine,
With all triumphant splendor on my brow;
But out alack, he was but one hour mine,
The region cloud hath masked him from me now.

Yet him for this my love no whit disdaineth;
Suns of the world may stain when heaven's sun
staineth.

PERFORMANCE SCRIPT #1

SONNET 68
The two gravedigger/friends
proceed to Sonnet 68 trading
lines back and forth, grieving
for their friend, as they relieve
him of his wallet, hat, boots,
whatever.)

GRAVEDIGGER ONE
Thus is his cheek the map of days outworn;
When beauty lived and died as flowers do now,

GRAVEDIGGER TWO
Before these bastard signs of fair were born,

GRAVEDIGGER ONE
Or durst inhabit on a living brow;

GRAVEDIGGER TWO
Before the golden tresses of the dead,
The right of sepulchers, were shorn away
To live a second life on second head,

GRAVEDIGGER ONE
Ere beauty's dead fleece made another gay.

GRAVEDIGGER TWO
In him whose holy antique hours are seen,
Without all ornament, itself and true,

GRAVEDIGGER ONE
Making no summer of another's green,

GRAVEDIGGER TWO
Robbing no old to dress his beauty new;

SHAKESPEARE SONNETS AS SCENES

                    GRAVEDIGGER ONE
And him as for a map doth Nature store,
To show false Art what beauty was of yore.

        ("Dead" body awakens, sits up, grabs
        his wallet back as gravediggers,
        horrified run off. "Dead" body now
        passes out again with a smile on his
        face.)

                        NARRATOR
What happens when two suitors vie for the same person? Well, sonnets 18, 141, 147, and 120 tell the story.

                    SONNET 18
                        LADY
                    (to Suitor One)
Shall I compare thee to a summer's day?
Thou art more lovely and more temperate.
Rough winds do shake the darling buds of May,
And summer's lease hath all too short a date.

                        LADY
                    (to Suitor Two)
Sometime two hot the eye of heaven shines,
And often is his gold complexion dimmed;
And every fair from fair sometime declines,
By chance, or by Nature's changing course, untrimmed.

                        LADY
                    (to Suitor One)
    But thy eternal summer shall not fade,
  Nor lose possession of that fair thou ow'st,

PERFORMANCE SCRIPT #1

                    LADY
                (to Suitor Two)
Nor shall Death brag thou wand'rest in his shade,
When in eternal lines to time thou grow'st.

                    LADY
                 (to herself)
So long as men can breathe or eyes can see,
So long lives this and this gives life

                    LADY
               (to third Suitor who
           appears at the last minute.)
to thee.

        (Lady leaves with new suitor leaving
        Suitors One and Two to lament not
        being the one chosen.)

        (As the suitors trade lines they each
        try to top the other in their grief.
        One through his anger, the other
        through his sadness.)

                SONNETS 141 & 147
                    SUITOR ONE
              (To girl who has just left
                  with new suitor.)
In faith I do not love thee with mine eyes,
For they in thee a thousand errors note;
But 'tis my heart that loves what they despise,
Who in spite of view is pleased to dote.

SHAKESPEARE SONNETS AS SCENES

SUITOR TWO
(To girl who has just left
with new suitor.)
My love is as a fever longing still,
For that which longer nurseth the disease;
Feeding on that which doth preserve the ill,
The uncertain sickly appetite to please.

SUITOR ONE
(Tries to top rival.)
Nor are mine ears with thy tongue's tune delighted;
Nor tender feeling, to base touches prone,
Nor taste, not smell, desire to be invited
To any sensual feast with the alone:

SUITOR TWO
(Tries to top rival.
My reason, the physician to my love,
Angry that his prescriptions are not kept,
Hath left me, and I desperate now approve
Desire id death, which physic did except.

SUITOR ONE
(Now it's a back and forth.)
But my five wits nor my five senses can
Dissuade one foolish heart from serving thee,
Who leaves unswayed the likeness of a man,
Thy proud heart's slave and vassal wretch to be:

SUITOR TWO
(The bout continues)
Past cure I am, now Reason is part care,
And frantic-mad with evermost unrest;

PERFORMANCE SCRIPT #1

My thought and discourse as madmen's are,
At random from the truth vainly expressed;

              SUITOR ONE
          (The bout heightens)
Only my plague thus far I count my gain,

              SUITOR TWO
         (But running out of steam)
For I have sworn thee fair, and thought thee bright,

              SUITOR ONE
       (Also tired of this game)
That she that makes me sin awards me pain.

              SUITOR TWO
Who art as black as hell, as dark as night.

    (As suitors sink back to their
    private despair, the lady and her
    new lover enter apparently having a
    lover's spat. Both suitors listen
    intently, hoping the couple breaks
    up, cheering on the girl as she
    berates her new lover, until the
    final couplet where the suitors see
    all hope disappear.)

              SONNET 120
                LADY
That you were once unkind befriends me now,
And for that sorrow which I then did feel

              SUITOR THREE
Needs must I under my transgression bow,
Unless my nerves were brass or hammered steel.

SHAKESPEARE SONNETS AS SCENES

LADY
For if you were by my unkindness shaken,
As I by yours, y'have passed a hell of time,

SUITOR THREE
And I, a tyrant, have no leisure taken
To weigh how once I suffered in your crime.

LADY
O, that our night of woe might have rememb'red
My deepest sense how hard true sorrow hits,

SUITOR THREE
And soon to you, as you to me then, tend'red
The humble salve which wounded bosoms fits!
But that your trespass now becomes a fee;

LADY
Mine ransoms yours, and yours must ransom me.

> (The couple kiss passionately and head off, presumably to be alone for their lovemaking. The rejected suitors walk off together in the opposite direction presumably to the pub to drink their sorrows away.)

Note: If both Performance Scripts #1 and #2 are to be done together, skip the next section, and go directly to Script #2.

NARRATOR
> (As Narrator is saying this next, final speech, the rest of the actors move on stage into positions to end the program with Sonnet 74.)

PERFORMANCE SCRIPT #1

Next time you read a sonnet, which you will as soon as you can google one, right? See what story you can create from those mere fourteen lines into your very own sonnet as a scene. Until we meet again… Sonnet 74.

SONNET 74
ALL/ENSEMBLE

ACTOR ONE
But be contented. When that fell arrest
Without all bail shall carry me (us) away,

ACTOR TWO
My (our) life hath in this line some interest
Which for memorial still with thee shall stay.

ACTOR THREE
When thou reviewest this, thou doth review
The very part was consecrate to thee.

ACTOR FOUR
The earth can have but earth, which is his due;
My (our) spirit is thine, the better part of me (we).

ACTOR FIVE
So then thou hast but lost the dregs of life,
The prey of worms, my (our) body being dead;

ACTOR SIX
The coward conquest of a wretch's knife,
Too base of thee to be remembered.

ALL
The worth of that is that which it contains,
And that is this, and this with thee remains.

THE END

APPENDIX C

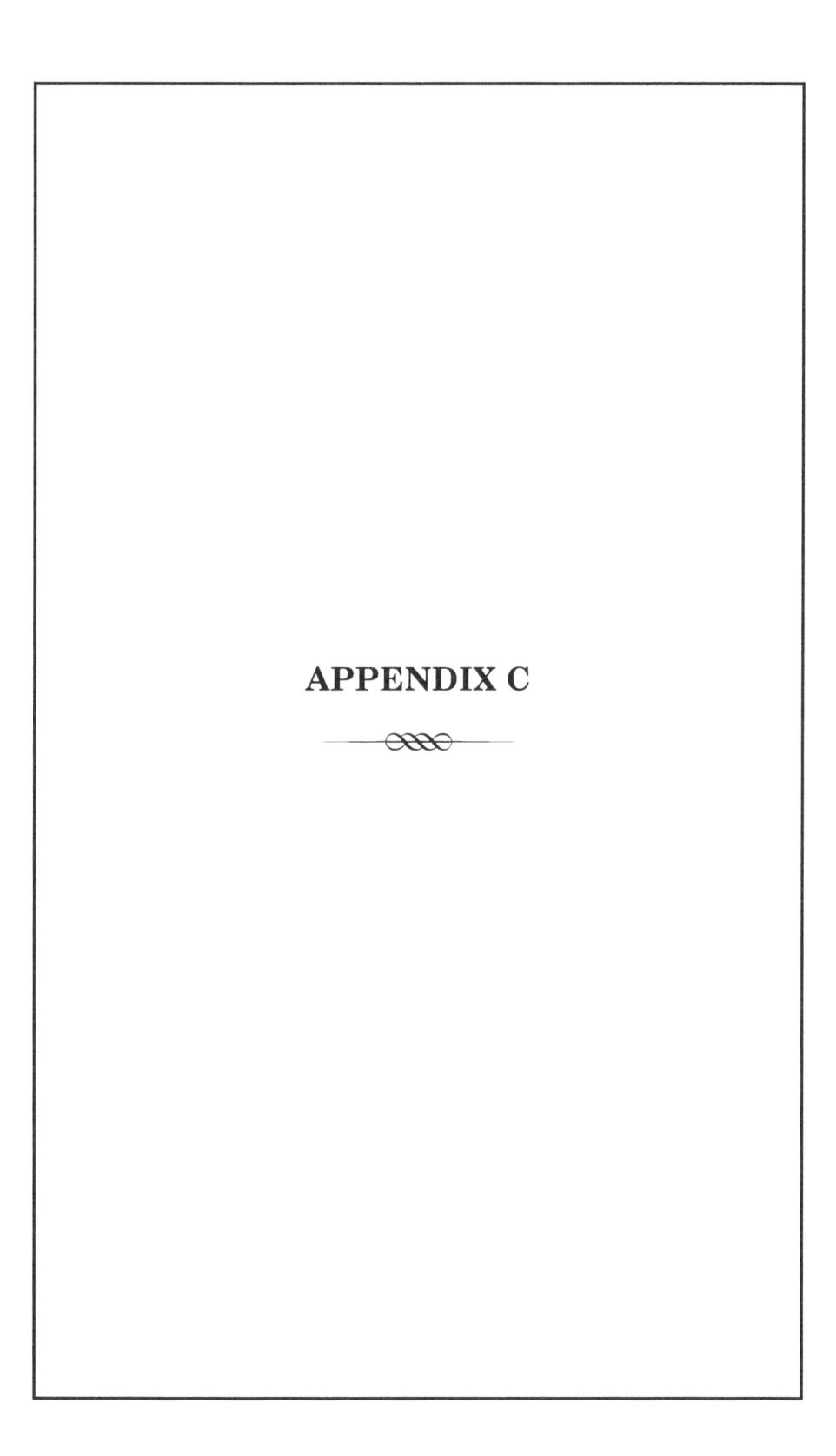

SHAKESPEARE
SONNETS AS SCENES

―――――――――――――――

"Performance Script #2"

SHAKESPEARE SONNETS AS SCENES

"Cast of Characters"

Sonnets: 14, 26, 74, 75, 116, 128

Length: approximately 35 minutes

Suggested Cast: 6-8 actors including Narrator
Parts to be decided between the actors and their director

Props: book of sonnets (Narrator), food in a box (Sonnet 75), letter (Sonnet 26), musical instrument (Sonnet 128), cloak for bride (Sonnet 116)

Costumes: limited only by the creativity of the actors

This script can be combined with Performance Script #1 for a longer presentation.

*See Appendix E in Sonnets As Scenes, The Sonnet as a Storytelling Device, for each sonnet with its text and subtext.

"PERFORMANCE SCRIPT #2"

NARRATOR

We are now in a world where poetry is not poetry but words telling a short story. Shakespeare wrote 154 poems in sonnet form consisting of only fourteen lines each. His words may sound funny to us, but many of them probably sounded funny to Shakespeare's 16th century audiences as well, because Shakespeare made up many of his words. Some words we use today because of Shakespeare are:

PERFORMANCE SCRIPT #2

> (Words are said separately by
> each of the ensemble members.)

ENSEMBLE
Amazement, Assassination, Bloody, Frugal, Generous, Laughable, Majestic, Obscene, Radiance, Road, Suspicious.

NARRATOR
Shakespeare also brought words together to create new phrases:

> (Phrases are said separately
> By each of the ensemble members.)

ENSEMBLE
Fight fire with fire, Set your teeth on edge, Heart of gold, Good riddance, Seen better days, Wear your heart on your sleeve, The game is up, Green-eyed monster, Vanish into thin air.

NARRATOR
A sonnet can certainly stand on its own. With a little help from our imaginations we can see a sonnet as a scene with one character telling its story.

> (as Narrator flips through
> a book, actor gets into place)

NARRATOR
Sonnet 75 is a sonnet as a simple scene!

SONNET 75
FOODIE
So are you to my thoughts as food is to life,
As sweet-seasoned showers are to the ground;

And for the peace of you I hold such strife
As 'twixt a miser and his wealth is found;

Now proud as an enjoyer, and anon
Doubting the filching age will stead his treasure;
Now counting best to be with you alone,
Then bettered that the world may see my pleasure;

Sometime too full of feasting on your sight,
And by and by clean starv-ed for a look;
Possessing or pursuing no delight
Save what is had or must from you be took.

Thus do I pine and surfeit day by day,
Or gluttoning on all, or all away.

                    NARRATOR
And now a sonnet with two characters. Sonnet 26

            (Soldier at attention)
                SONNET 26
            SOLDIER'S LOVE INTEREST
        (Girl trying to get soldier at
        attention to notice her, leaves him
        a note. After she leaves he breaks
        attention, picks it up, kisses it,
        then quickly puts it in his pocket
        and goes back to attention.)

Lord of my love, to whom in vassalage
Thy merit hath my duty strongly knit,
To thee I send this written ambassage,
To witness duty, not to show my wit.

PERFORMANCE SCRIPT #2

Duty so great, which wit so poor as mine
May make seem bare, in wanting words to show it,
But that I hope some good conceit of thine
In thy soul's thought, all naked, with bestow it;

Till whatsoever star that guides my moving
Points on me graciously with fair aspect,
And puts apparel on my tottered loving
To show me worthy of thy sweet respect.

Then may I dare to boast how I do love thee;
Till then, not show my head where thou mayst prove me.

                  NARRATOR
           (Flipping through book.)
Here's another one, Sonnet 128. We add a musician, his music, and groupies. Yes, there were groupies in Shakespeare's time.

                  SONNET 128
             MUSICIAN WITH GROUPIES
    (Musician playing the end of "Greensleeves," leaving his guitar on chair by mistake when he leaves with his groupies, except one who stays behind and directs her love for him to his guitar. After sonnet musician returns with groupies to collect his guitar never noticing her.)

SHAKESPEARE SONNETS AS SCENES

FAN

How oft, when thou, my (your) music, music play'st,
Upon that blessed wood whose motion sounds
With thy sweet fingers when thou gently sway'st
The wiry concord that mine ear confounds.

Do I envy those jacks that nimble leap
To kiss the tender inward of thy hand,
Whilst my poor lips, which should that harvest reap,
At the wood's boldness by thee (my) blushing stand.

To be so tickled, they would change their state
And situation with those dancing chips
O'er whom thy fingers walk with gentle gait,
Making dead wood more blest than living lips.

Since saucy jacks so happy are in this,
Give them thy fingers, me thy lips to kiss.

NARRATOR

"If music be the food of love, play on!"

> (From Twelfth Night: Act1/Scene1
> Narrator can choose to tell audience
> the source of the quote or not.)

Of course, you can put sonnets together with other dialogue to create a mini-play. We present an epic wedding ensemble scene, Sonnet 116 paired with Sonnet 14 and the witches from Macbeth.

This is really thinking outside the box. Shakespeare would be so proud!

PERFORMANCE SCRIPT #2

                    WITCHES
              (Macbeth Act 1/Scene 1)

                    WITCH 1
When will we three meet again? In thunder, lightning or in rain?

                    WITCH 2
When the hurly-burly's done. When the battle's lost and won.

                    WITCH 3
That will be ere the set of sun.

                    WITCH 1
Where the place?

                    WITCH 2
Upon the heath.

                    WITCH 3
There to meet with Macbeth.

                      ALL
Fair is foul, and foul is fair; hover through the fog and filthy air.

                   SONNET 14
   (The witches see a young girl,
   with a cloak covering her body,
   crying. They surround her and
   trading lines in Sonnet 14. Tell
   her fortune. Afterwards,they
   hear the crowd coming and they
   exit, leaving the girl alone.)

SHAKESPEARE SONNETS AS SCENES

                    WITCH ONE
Not from the stars do I my judgment pluck
And yet me thinks I have astronomy;
But not to tell of good or evil luck,
Of plagues, of dearths, or seasons' quality.

                    WITCH TWO
Nor can I fortune to brief minutes tell,
Pointing to each his thunder, rain, and wind,
Or say with princes if it should go well
By oft predict that I in heaven find.

                    WITCH THREE
But from thine eyes my knowledge I derive,
And, constant stars, in them I read such art
As truth and beauty shall together thrive
If from thyself to store thou wouldst convert;

                    WITCH ONE
Or else of the this I (we) prognosticate,

                    WITCH TWO
Thy end is truth's and beauty's

                    WITCH THREE
Doom and date.

                    SONNET 116
            WEDDING GUESTS, BRIDE, GROOM,
               BRIDE'S FATHER, PREACHER
            (Wedding – ensemble piece, with
            interspersed dialogue. Young girl
            and young man attempt to be wed.)

PERFORMANCE SCRIPT #2

PREACHER
Dearly beloved, if anyone here has just cause why these two young people should not be married, let them speak now or forever hold their peace.

WEDDING GUEST
Let me not to the marriage of true minds
Admit impediments; love is not love
Which alters when it alteration finds,
Or bend with the remover to remove.

PREACHER
Thank you. If anyone here has just cause why these two young people should not be married, let them…

WEDDING GUEST
O, no, it is an ever fix-ed mark
That looks on tempests and is never shaken'
It is the star to ever wand'ring bark,
Whose worth's unknown although his height be taken.

PREACHER
May I continue? If anyone…

WEDDING GUEST
Love's not Time's fool, though rosy lips and cheeks
Within his bending sickle's compass come;
Love alters not with his brief hours and weeks,
But bears it out even to the edge of doom.

> (There is a cry from the bride who is going into labor. She is rushed off by her father and the groom.)

SHAKESPEARE SONNETS AS SCENES

                    PREACHER
             (following them out)
Say "I do!" Say "I do!"

                    BRIDE
I do!

                    GROOM
I do!

                    PREACHER
I now pronounce you man and wife!

    (Off stage we hear a Baby cry.)

             OTHER WEDDING GUESTS
    (Big collective sigh of relief
    and happiness.)

                 WEDDING GUEST
If this be error and upon me proved,
I never writ, not no man ever loved.

                    NARRATOR
    (As the actors join the narrator
    on stage.)

We challenge you to read Shakespeare's sonnets and see which one tells you a story. Then memorize it and present it to your friends or classmates. You might just enjoy it!

                    SONNET 74
                  ENSEMBLE/ALL

PERFORMANCE SCRIPT #2

ACTOR ONE
But be contented. When that fell arrest
Without all bail shall carry me (us) away,

ACTOR TWO
My (our) life hath in this line some interest
Which for memorial still with thee shall stay.

ACTOR THREE
When thou reviewest this, thou doth review
The very part was consecrate to thee.

ACTOR FOUR
The earth can have but earth, which is his due;
My (our) spirit is thine, the better part of me (we).

ACTOR FIVE
So then thou hast but lost the dregs of life,
The prey of worms, my (our) body being dead;

ACTOR SIX
The coward conquest of a wretch's knife,
Too base of thee to be remembered.

ALL
The worth of that is that which it contains,
And that is this, and this with thee remains.

THE END

APPENDIX D

Sonnets Listed with Storylines

Following is a list of the thirty sonnets referenced in this book in numerical order. It lists the sonnet by 1) number 2) first line 3) main character 4) chapter(s) where sonnet is mentioned and/or discussed 5) sonnets it can be paired with 6) and a brief description of the storyline.

This is only a small fraction of the 154 sonnets Shakespeare wrote. Every sonnet has a story, or many stories, to tell limited only by the imagination of the storyteller.

Sonnets as Scenes with Storylines

Sonnet No.	First Line/Description	Brief Title	Chapter/Appendix	Pair with
3	"Now look in thy glass" Egotistical son rejects girl mother has chosen for him	Mother	5, A, B, C, D	62, 69
14	"Not from the stars" Three witches telling one person's fortune	Fortune Teller	5, 8, A, B, C, D	14, 116

67

SHAKESPEARE SONNETS AS SCENES

Sonnet No.	First Line/Description	Brief Title	Chapter/Appendix	Pair with
18	"Shall I compare thee"	Two Suitors	1, 2, 4, A, B, C, D	141, 147, 120
	Woman unsure which suitor to choose			
19	"Devouring Time, blunt thou the lion's paws"		3, A, B, C, D	
	Man, in hospital waiting room, waiting to hear if his loved one lives or dies			
26	"Lord of my love"	Valentine	2, 8, A, B, C, D	
	Girl trying to get a soldier's attention			
29	"When in disgrace with Fortune"	Love Poem	3, 7, A, B, C, D	
	Straightforward love poem			
33	"Full many a glorious morning"	Widow	1, 5, 7, A, B, C, D	68
	Widows: older one to her deceased older husband, younger one to her soldier husband killed in battle			
41	"Those pretty wrongs that liberty commits."	Boyfriend	2, A, B, C, D	
	Boyfriend spying on girlfriend he thinks is cheating on her			
43	"When most I wink"	Man and Fairy	3, A, B, C, D	
	Man who awakes to see a fairy and falls in love with her			
50	"Now heavy do I journey"	Boy and Girl	5, A, B, C, D	148
	Tired, spoiled girl insisting her boyfriend carry her			

SONNETS LISTED WITH STORYLINES

Sonnet No.	First Line/Description	Brief Title	Chapter/Appendix	Pair with
53	"What is your substance" Girl who dreams of a fairy friend	Girl and Fairy	2, A, B, C, D	
57	"Being your slave, what should I do but tend." Fool to his Queen	Fool	2, A, B, C, D	
62	"Sin of self-love" Egotistical son rejects mother's ply for girl of her choice	Son	5, A, B, C, D	3, 69
66	"Tir'd with all these" General and his troops surviving a losing battle or getting ready to go into battle	General	2, A, B, C, D	
68	"Thus is his cheek" Gravedigger's friend has died and they lament his passing	Grave Diggers	3, 5, 7, A, B, C, D	68
69	"Those parts of thee" Egotistical son rejects mother's ploy for girl of her choice	Girlfriend	5, A, B, C, D	
74	"But be contented" Use to end performance with all actors on the stage	Finale/ Ensemble	2, 7, 8, 10, A, B, C, D	
75	"So are you to my thoughts" Guy with box of food, maybe? Or girl praising a guy eating pizza, or so he thinks	Girl or Guy	1, 2, 3, 8, A, B, C, D	

69

SHAKESPEARE SONNETS AS SCENES

Sonnet No.	First Line/Description	Brief Title	Chapter/Appendix	Pair with
109	"O, never say" Man, as his dog lay dying	Dying Dog	2, A, B, C, D	
116	"Let me not to the marriage" Attempt to marry a pregnant woman to her lover	Wedding Guest	2, 5, 8, A, B, C, D 14	
120	"That you were once unkind" Girl with two suitors, having chosen a third, now arguing with him	Two Lovers	5, 7, A, B, C, D	18, 141, 147
128	"How of't when thou my music" Girl groupie tells of her love for a musician to his instrument	Groupie	2, 8, A, B, C, D	
130	"My mistress' eyes are nothing like the sun." Man complimenting his lady in awkward fashion	Man	2, 8, A, B C, D	
138	"When my love swears that he is made of truth." Older woman (cougar) to her young lover	Older Woman	2, A, B, C, D	
139	"O, call not me to justify" Man dying in battle with his trusty sword	Soldier	2, A, B, C, D	
141	"In faith I do not love thee" Rejected suitor angry he was not chosen	Suitor One	2, 5, 7, A, B, C, D	18, 147, 120
144	"Two loves I have" Guy finds wallet, debating with himself whether to return it or not	Guy	3, A, B, C, D	

SONNETS LISTED WITH STORYLINES

Sonnet No.	First Line/Description	Brief Title	Chapter/Appendix	Pair with
145	"Those lips that love's own hand"	Mother	2, A, B, C, D	
	Young girl tells mother she hates her, mother trying to talk to her			
147	"My love is a fever"	Suitor Two	5, 7, A, B, C, D	18, 141, 120
	Rejected suitor sad that he was not chosen			
148	"O me! What eyes hath love"	Nearsighted Guy	5, A, B, C, D	50
	Girl teases guy with his eyeglasses, he has trouble finding her			

APPENDIX E

Sonnets with Subtext

Following is a list of the thirty sonnets referenced in this book in numerical order with subtext.

These sonnets with subtext can be used as jumping off points in rehearsals. The subtexts are only suggestions. The actor may want to use different subtext in telling whatever story they choose.

Some of the sonnets do not have detailed subtext.

For reference: 1) Stage directions are in italics with parentheses. 2) The character's inner thoughts are under "Subtext" without italics or parentheses.

SHAKESPEARE SONNETS AS SCENES

SONNET 3
"Look in thy glass and tell the face thou viewest"

Cast: Young Man, Young Girl, Mother, Artist

Paired with Sonnets 62 and 69   1) Sonnet 69   2) Sonnet 3   3) Sonnet 62

1) Sonnet 69 is Young Girl trying to get the attention of the Young Man. 2) Sonnet 3 is the Young Man's Mother trying to get him to pay attention to the Young Girl. 3) Sonnet 62 begins after an Artist has offered to draw a picture of the Young Man. At the end of Sonnet 62 the artist shows a picture of a horse's ass. Mother and Young Girl find this hilarious.

MOTHER:	SUBTEXT
(Mother gives hand mirror to her son, the Young Man.)	
Look in thy glass and tell the face thou viewest	Get married, son. I want grandchildren.
Now is the time that face should form another, Whose fresh repair if now thou not renewest,	Do this while you are still young.
Thou dost beguile the world, unbless some mother.	If not, I will be very unhappy.
(Young Man is not really listening, just preening in the mirror.)	
For where is she so fair, whose uneared womb	Look at this girl I have found for you.
Distains the tillage of thy husbandry?	She will gladly accept you as her husband.
Or who is he so fond will be the tomb Of his self-love to stop posterity?	I am serious about this.
(Mother takes mirror from son and looks at herself in the mirror.) Turns out Mother is as vain as her son.	
Thou art thy mother's glass, and she in thee Calls back the lovely April of her prime; So thou through windows of thine age shalt see, Despite of wrinkles, this thy golden time.	

SONNETS WITH SUBTEXT

(Young Man/Son grabs mirror back from Mother.)
But if thou live rememb'red not to be,   I am exasperated with you;
                                         you will not listen!
Die single and thine image dies with thee.

(Mother exits with girl.)

*If Mini-Play: Artist enters and offers to draw the Young Man's picture.
Sonnet 62 begins.*

SHAKESPEARE SONNETS AS SCENES

SONNET 14
"Not from the stars do I my judgment pluck"

Cast: Fortune Teller

Paired with Sonnet 116: see Sonnet 14 with additional script from Macbeth.

FORTUNE TELLER:	SUBTEXT
(Fortune Teller picks someone from the audience to tell their fortune.)	
Not from the stars do I my judgment pluck,	I may be an astronomer.
And yet methinks I have astronomy;	
But not to tell of good or evil luck,	But not in the way you think.
Of plagues, of dearths, or seasons' quality;	
Nor can I fortune to brief minutes tell,	I cannot tell the weather.
Pointing to each his thunder, rain, and wind,	
Or say with princes if it shall go well	I cannot predict the fate of royalty.
By oft predict that I in heaven find.	
But from thine eyes my knowledge I derive,	It is what I see in your eyes.
And, constant stars, in them I read such art	I see all there is to see.
As truth and beauty shall together thrive	
If from thyself to store thou wouldst convert:	You will live a beautiful life IF you have children.
Or else of thee this I prognosticate,	If not…
Thy end is truth's and beauty's doom and date.	there is no future for you.

SONNETS WITH SUBTEXT

SONNET 14 with Macbeth
"Not from the stars do I my judgment pluck"

Cast: Three Witches, Young Girl

Paired with Sonnet 116: 1) Act One/Scene 1 Macbeth   2) Sonnet 14   3) Sonnet 116.

Girl with cloak covering her whole body in on stage with her back to the audience. Witches enter with Act One Scene One from Macbeth.

WITCH ONE:
When will we three meet again?
In thunder, lightning, or in rain?

WITCH TWO:
When the hurly-burly's done.
When the battle's lost and won.

WITCH THREE:
That will be ere the set of sun.

WITCH ONE:
Where the place?

WITCH TWO:
Upon the heath.

WITCH THREE:
There to meet with Macbeth.

ALL:
Fair is foul, and foul is fair; hover through
the fog and filthy air.

(The witches see a young girl with a cloak covering her body, crying. They surround her and tell her fortune.)
WITCH ONE:
Not from the stars do I my judgment pluck,

77

And yet methinks I have astronomy;
But not to tell of good or evil luck,
Of plagues, of dearths, or seasons' quality;

WITCH TWO:
Nor can I fortune to brief minutes tell,
Pointing to each his thunder, rain, and wind,
Or say with princes if it shall go well
By oft predict that I in heaven find.

WITCH THREE:
But from thine eyes my knowledge I derive,
And, constant stars, in them I read such art
As truth and beauty shall together thrive
If from thyself to store thou wouldst convert:

WITCH ONE:
Or else of thee this I prognosticate,

WITCH TWO:
Thy end is truth's and beauty's

WITCH THREE:
doom and date.

(As the wedding crowd approaches for Sonnet 116, the witches exit.)

SONNETS WITH SUBTEXT

SONNET 18
"Shall I compare thee to a summer's day?"

Cast: Lady Fair, Two Suitors, Handsome Man

*Paired with Sonnets 120, 141 and 147   1) Sonnet 18   2) Sonnets 141 and 147
3) Sonnet 120*

Lady Fair and Handsome Man exit leaving two jilted suitors. They trade Sonnets 141 and 147 back and forth lamenting that they weren't chosen. After which, Lady Fair and Handsome Man reenter arguing with Sonnet 120. She thinks he has wronged her; he cannot understand what he did wrong. They fight, but in the end, make-up still very much in love, and exit together to the disappointment of the two suitors.

LADY FAIR:	SUBTEXT
(Sitting on bench to Suitor One kneeling to her side.)	
Shall I compare thee to a summer's day?	Ah, yes, thou art fine indeed.
Thou art more lovely and more temperate.	
Rough winds do shake the darling buds of May,	Maybe you are too young for me.
And summer's lease hath all too short a date.	

LADY FAIR:

(To Suitor Two, who has entered and kneels to her left.)

Sometime too hot the eye of heaven shines,	My goodness how sexy!
And often is his gold complexion dimmed;	
And every fair from fair sometime declines,	Maybe a bit too sexy. That can't last.
By chance, or by nature's changing course, untrimmed.	

LADY FAIR:

(Back to Suitor One.)

But thy eternal summer shall not fade,	Maybe I spoke too soon, you are sexy, too.
Nor lose possession of the fair thou ow'st.	

LADY FAIR:

(Back to Suitor Two.)

Nor shall death brag thou wand'rest in his shade, Then again, you may keep up.
When in eternal lines to Time thou grow'st.

LADY FAIR:

(Stands, trying to make up her mind between the two.)

So long as men can breathe, or eyes can see, Oh, dear. Who to choose?
So long live this, and this gives life to… I'll give my heart to…

LADY FAIR:

(Handsome Man walks across stage and Lady Fair sees him.)

Thee! (Him!)

(Lady Fair exits with Handsome Man, leaving the two suitors crestfallen.)

SONNET 19
"Devouring Time, blunt thou the lion's paws"

Cast: Person (lover, parent, sibling, best friend – actor chooses) and Doctor

PERSON:	SUBTEXT
(Person in hospital waiting room, pleading with Time/God to do his worst, just not to their love who is in the operating room following an emergency illness/accident.)	
Devouring Time, blunt thou the lion's paws,	God/Time, you can do each of the following three
And make the earth devour her own sweet brood;	things to whomever you wish.
Pluck the keen teeth from the fierce tiger's jaws,	
And burn the long-live phoenix in her blood;	
Make glad and sorry seasons as thou fleets,	
And do whate'er thou wilt, swift-footed Time.	
To the wide world and all her fading sweets;	
But I forbid thee one most heinous crime,	BUT – do not do anything like that to my love, in any way.
O, carve not with thy hours my love's fair brow,	
Nor draw no lines there with thine antique pen;	
Him in thy course untainted do allow,	I simply won't allow it.
For beauty' pattern to succeeding men.	
Yet do thy worst, old Time; despite thy wrong,	Go ahead, do everything else, but please…
(Doctor comes in, shakes his head, and the person knows their loved one didn't make it.)	
My love shall in my verse ever live young.	Oh, my dear, I will love you forever.

SONNET 26
"Lord of my love, to whom in vassalage"

Cast: Young Girl, Soldier

YOUNG GIRL:	SUBTEXT
(Young Girl, in love with a soldier, has written him a love letter. She tries to get his attention, but because he is on guard and at attention, he cannot respond to him.)	
Lord of my love, to whom in vassalage	
Thy merit hath my duty strongly knit,	
To thee I send this written embassage,	
To witness duty, not to show my wit.	
She shows the letter to the soldier.	
Duty so great, which wit so poor as mine	I may not be a good writer but, my love for you
May make seem bare, in wanting words to show it,	makes me write this.
But that I hope some good conceit of thing	I am so hoping you feel the same.
In thy soul's thought, all naked, will bestow it.	
Till whatsoever star that guides my moving	I am ready to give my whole self to you.
Points on me graciously with fair aspect	
And puts apparel on my tottered loving,	
To show me worthy of thy sweet respect.	
Then may I dare to board how I do love thee;	Oh, I've tried everything to get you to notice me.
Til then, not show my head where thou mays prove me.	I will not bother you again.
(As she exits, she releases the letter and it floats to the ground in front of the soldier. The soldier breaks attention, picks up the letter, lovingly looks at it, hides it in his jacket, and goes back to attention.)	

SONNET 29
"When in disgrace with Fortune and men's eyes"

Cast: If paired with Sonnet 33 - Soldier, Young Wife

As a Stand Alone: no subtext needed; it speaks for itself.

Paired with Sonnet 33: Lights up on one side of stage. We see a soldier reading aloud a letter he has written to his wife back home. After sonnet, lights go down on the soldier and come up on other side of stage on his wife having just read his letter. She is happy. She picks up the next letter in her lap to read that her husband has been killed in the line of duty.

SOLDIER:
When in disgrace with Fortune and men's eyes,
I all alone beweep my outcast state,
And trouble deaf heaven with my bootless cries,
And look upon myself and curse my fate.

Wishing me like to one more rich in hope,
Featured like him, like him with friends possessed,
Desiring this man's art, and that man's scope,
With what I most enjoy contented least;

Yet in these thoughts myself almost despising,
Haply I think on thee, and then my state,
Like to the lark at break of day arising
From sullen earth, sings hymns at heaven's gate;

For thy sweet love rememb'red such wealth brings,
That then I scorn to change my state with kings.

SHAKESPEARE SONNETS AS SCENES

SONNET 33
"Full many a glorious morning have I seen"

Cast: Widow

Paired with Sonnet 14: A very sad girl, possibly upset by a boyfriend dumping her, or a widow, after which the witches see her and come to her with the predictions in Sonnet 14.

Paired with Sonnet 29: Soldier on battlefield writing a love letter to his young wife. His young wife, after reading his letter, picks up another letter and reads that her husband, the soldier, has been killed in battle.

Paired with Sonnet 68: Widow at her husband's casket saying goodbye in a very big and vocal way surrounded by her husband's two friends who happen to be the gravediggers. They are all over the top, crying and wailing.

WIDOW:	SUBTEXT
Full many a glorious morning have I seen Flatter the mountain tops with sovereign eye, Kissing with golden face the meadows green, Gilding pale streams with heavenly alchemy;	Our love affair was glorious!
Anon permit the basest clouds to ride	So quickly, without my consent, my love was taken from me.
With ugly rack on his celestial face, And from the forlorn world his visage hide,	His killer has run away and hidden himself.
Stealing unseen to west with this disgrace.	
Even so my sun one early morn did shine,	When he was alive, he was magnificent.
With all triumphant splendor on my brow; But out alack, he was but one hour mine,	Oh, my love is gone and our time was too short.
The region cloud hath masked him from me now.	
Yet him for this my love no whit disdaineth;	Even so, I do not blame the living.
Suns of the world may stain when heaven's sun staineth.	They cannot compare to my love, even though he is gone.

84

SONNETS WITH SUBTEXT

SONNET 41
"Those pretty wrongs that liberty commits"

Cast: Young Man, His Girlfriend, A Stranger

YOUNG MAN:

(Girlfriend is waiting for someone. Hidden from her is her boyfriend, who suspects she is cheating on him. Enter a man. Girlfriend and man embrace, clearly knowing each other. They begin to chat quietly as Young Man/boyfriend comes forward to say sonnet.)

	SUBTEXT
Those pretty wrongs that liberty commits,	Oh, no. She has found someone else.
When I am sometime absent from thy heart,	
Thy beauty and thy years full well befits,	
For still temptation follows where thou art.	
Gentle thou art, and therefore to be won;	He has won her heart.
Beauteous thou art, therefore to be assailed;	
And when a woman woos, what woman's son	Look at the way he hugged her.
Will sourly leave her till she have prevailed?	This must have been going on for a while.
Ay me, but yet thou might'st my seat forbear,	He's not that good-looking.
And chide thy beauty and thy straying youth,	
Who lead thee in their riot even there	What does he have that I don't have?
Where thou art forced to break a twofold truth;	
Hers, by thy beauty tempting her to thee,	She is so beautiful.
Thine, by thy beauty being false to me.	But she is a cheater.

(The girl turns around and sees her boyfriend.)
GIRLFRIEND:
Sweetheart! Come here and meet my brother.

SONNET 43
"When most I wink, then do mine eyes best see"

Cast: Young Man and Fairy

YOUNG MAN: SUBTEXT
(Sleeping Young Man awaken by a fairy.)

When most I wink, then do mine eyes best see,   Do I see what I think I see?
For all the day they view things unrespected,
But when in sleep, in dreams they look on thee   I must be dreaming.
And, darkly bright, are bright in dark directed.

Then thou, whose shadow shadows doth make bright,   I am so happy to see you.
How would thy shadow's form form happy show
To the clear day with thy much clearer light,   I am so happy to be with you.
When to unseeing eyes thy shade shines so!

How would, I say, mine eyes be blessed made,   If I could only see you when I am awake.

By looking on thee in the living day,
When in dead night thy fair imperfect shade   But in sleep you are all mine.
Through heavy sleep on sightless eyes doth stay!

All days are nights to see till I see thee,   And so I shall sleep to be with you.

And nights bright days when dreams do show thee me.

SONNET 50
"How heavy do I journey on the way"

Cast: Girl, Boy

The couple have been walking a long distance with a long way yet to go. They are tired. Being a good boyfriend, the boy picks up the girl and carries her piggyback style.

GIRL:
How heavy do I journey on the way
When what I seek, my weary travel's end,
Doth teach that ease and that repose to say,
"Thus far the miles are measured from thy friend.

(He's having trouble. He is tired and she is heavy. She is encouraging him to go faster.)

GIRL:
The beast that bears me, tired with my woe,
Plods dully on, to bear that weight in me,
As if by some instinct the wretch did know
His rider loved not speed, being made from thee.

(He tries to go faster, but is not happy that she keeps kicking him.)

GIRL:
The bloody spur cannot provoke him on,
That sometimes anger thrusts his hide,
Which heavily he answers with a groan,
More sharp to me than spurring to his side;

(Boy is fed up with trying to please her. He drops her on the ground.)

BOY:
For that same groan doth put this in my mind:
My grief lies onward and my joy behind.

(He exits.)

SHAKESPEARE SONNETS AS SCENES

SONNET 50/148
"How heavy do I journey on the way"
"O me, what eyes hath Love put in my heart"

Cast: Two Boys and Two Girls

At end of these dual scenes is an alternate ending.

Scene begins with Sonnet 148. Guy with glasses and his girlfriend, who has taken his glasses and not he can't see.

BOY WITH GLASSES (SONNET 148)   SUBTEXT

His girlfriend has taken his glasses and is teasing him to come find her. He is having trouble navigating without them.)

O me, what eyes hath Love put in my head,
Which have no correspondence with true sight!
Or, if they have, where is my judgment fled,
That censures falsely what they see aright?

(As second couple enter, first couple freezes.)

(Second couple have walked a long way with a long way to go. They are tired. The boyfriend picks up his girlfriend, piggyback style, to carry her.)

GIRL: (SONNET 50)
How heavy do I journey on the way
When what I seek, my weary travel's end,
Doth teach that ease and that repose to say,
"Thus far the miles are measured from my friend."

(They exit.)

BOY: (SONNET 148)

(Girlfriend sneaks up on him, offers him the glasses, then snatches them back from him.)

It that be fair whereon my false eyes dote,
What means the world to say it is not so?
If it be not, then love doth well denote
Love's eye is not so true as all men's no.

88

(*Each time Piggyback couple reenter, first couple stops to watch them.*)

GIRL: (SONNET 50)

The beast that bears me, tired with my woe,
Plods dully on to bear that weight in me,

(*She's encouraging her boyfriend to go faster.*)

As if by some instinct the wretch did know
His rider loved not speed, being made from thee.

(*The exit again.*)

(*Girlfriend resumes teasing her boyfriend with his glasses.*)

BOY (SONNET 148)

How can it be? O, how can Love's eye be true,
That is so vexed then though I mistake my view;

Maybe she's not such a good girlfriend. I'm beginning to see that now.

The sun itself see not till heaven clears.

(*Piggyback couple reenters. The boy is very tired and very angry with his girlfriend's nagging.*)

GIRL: (SONNET 50)

The bloody spur cannot provoke him on,
That sometimes anger thrusts into his hide,
Which heavily he answers with a groan,
More sharp to me than spurring to his side;

(*He has had enough and dumps her on the ground.*)

BOY: (SONNET 50)

(*His last words to her as he exits.*)

For that same groan doth put this in my mind:
My grief lies onward and my joy behind.

(*She gets up and follows him off.*)

*(Girlfriend (Sonnet 148) gives the glasses back to
her boyfriend with a kiss on the cheek.)*

BOY (SONNET 148)

O cunning Love, with tears thou keep'st me blind,   I am lucky to have her and
                                                                           not that other girl.

Lest eyes well-seeing thy foul faults should find.

*(Happy now with his glasses on he takes his girlfriend
into his arms and gives her a good kiss on the lips.)*

*ALTERNATE ENDING: The piggyback boyfriend dumps his girlfriend in between
the first couple. She sits there bewildered. The boy (Sonnet 148) is now impatient
to get his glasses back, reaches for them and falls over piggyback girl. They make
eye contact and the glasses boy quickly decides that piggyback girl is better than the
glasses girl He helps the piggyback girl up and onto his back as she gives him directions and they exit together, leaving the first girl alone with only a pair of glasses*

SONNET 53
"What is your substance, whereof are you made?"

Cast: Sleeping Girl and Fairy

SLEEPING GIRL:	SUBTEXT
(Sleeping Girl awakened by fairy.)	
What is your substance, whereof are you made,	There is something here?
That millions of strange shadows on you tend?	
Since everyone hath, every one, one shade;	I think I see you there.
And you, but one, can every shadow lend.	
Describe Adonis, and the counterfeit	I can't believe how beautiful you are.
Is poorly imitated after you;	More than Adonis.
On Helen's cheek all art of beauty set,	More than Helen.
And you in Grecian tires are painted new.	
Speak of the spring and foison of the year;	I am in love with you.
The one doth shadow of your beauty show,	
The other at your bounty doth appear,	But I can't touch you.
And you in every blessed shape we know.	Wait! What?
In all eternal grace you have some part,	
But you like none, none you, for constant heart.	I am sure I will see you soon in my dreams.

SONNET 57
"Being your slave, what should I do but tend"

Cast: Jester

<u>JESTER:</u>
(Jester, in a moment of quiet, to his Queen.)
Being your slave, what should I do but tend
Upon the hours and times of your desire?
I have no precious time at all to spend,
Nor services to do till you require.

Nor dare I chide the world-without-end hour
Whilst I, my sovereign, watch the clock for you,
Nor think of bitterness of absence sour
When you have bid your servant once adieu.

Nor dare I question with my jealous thought
Where you may be, or your affairs suppose,
But, like a sad slave, stay and thing of naught
Save where you are how happy you make those.

So true a fool is love that in your will,
Though you do anything, he thinks no ill.

SONNETS WITH SUBTEXT

SONNET 62
"Those parts of thee that the world's eye doth view"

Cast: Young Man, Young Girl, Mother, Artist

Paired with Sonnets 3 and 69   1) Sonnet 69   2) Sonnet 3   3) Sonnet 62

1) Sonnet 69 is Young Girl trying to get the attention of the Young Man. 2) Sonnet 3 is the Young Man's Mother trying to get him to pay attention to the Young Girl. 3) Sonnet 62 begins after an Artist has offered to draw a picture of the Young Man. At the end of Sonnet 62 the artist shows a picture of a horse's ass. Mother and Young Girl find this hilarious.

YOUNG MAN:	SUBTEXT
(Looking at himself in a hand-held mirror and admiring himself.)	
Sin of self-love possesseth all mine eye	
And all my soul and all my ever part;	
And for this sin there is no remedy,	
It is so grounded inward in my heart.	
(Possibly a hair is out of place; he puts is back.)	
Methinks no face so gracious is as mine,	My face is so beautiful.
No shape so true, no truth of such account,	My body is so sexy.
And for myself mine own worth do define,	If I say so myself.
As I all other in all worths surmount.	I am the best looking of all.
But when my glass shows me myself indeed,	Even when I am old.
Beated and chopped with tanned antiquity,	
Mine own self-love quite contrary I read;	I will still be gorgeous.
Self so self-loving were iniquity.	There is no doubt to that.
'Tis thee, myself, that for myself I praise,	I love me!
Painting my age with beauty of thy days.	Young or old there is no one a beautiful as me!

(Young Man exits very pleased with himself.)

If Mini-Play: At end of sonnet artist shows drawing of a horse's ass. Mother and Young Girl find his very funny. The Young Man does not.

SHAKESPEARE SONNETS AS SCENES

SONNET 66
"Tired with all these, for restful death I cry"

Cast: General and Three Soldiers

GENERAL:
(General and his troops, tired from battle, enter and line up for inspection. All are clearly exhausted. The General takes a deep breath, preparing to inspect his troops.)

He walks down the line, with an effort, inspecting his soldiers.

Tired with all these, for restful death I cry,
As, to behold desert a beggar born,
And needy nothing trimmed in jollity,
And purest faith unhappily forsworn,

(General goes to first soldier and excuses him. The solider sits.)

And gilded honor shamefully misplaced,
And maiden virtue rudely strumpeted,

(General goes to second soldier and excuses him. The soldier sits.)

And right perfection wrongly disgraced,
And strength by limping sway disabled,

(General goes to third man and excuses him.)

And art made tongue-tied by authority,
And folly (doctorlike) controlling skill,

(Third man falls into his arms. General gently helps him sit.)

And simple truth miscalled simplicity,
And captive good attending captain ill.

(General sits and takes out a photo of his loved one., placing it close to his heart.)

Tired with all these, from these would I be gone,
Save that to die, I leave my love alone.

SHAKESPEARE SONNETS AS SCENES

SONNET 68
"Thus is his cheek the map of days outworn"

Cast: Two Gravediggers, One Dead Body

Paired with Sonnet 33: the scene begins with the Gravediggers bringing in the body of their deceased friend and laying him on the ground. The widow is there and says Sonnet 33 as a goodbye to her husband. The gravediggers keep interrupting her with their own crying. She finishes and leaves but not without giving them a stern look.

GRAVEDIGGER ONE:	SUBTEXT
(Two Gravediggers bring a "dead" body on stage preparing to bury their friend. As they cry over their friend, they notice he has nice things. They start to relieve the body of its hat, belt, watch, etc.)	
Thus is his cheek the map of days outworn,	
When beauty lived and died as flowers do now,	
GRAVEDIGGER TWO:	
Before these bastard signs of fair were born,	
GRAVEDIGGER ONE:	
Or durst inhabit on a living brow;	Nice scarf. He won't need it.
GRAVEDIGGER TWO:	
Before the golden tresses of the dead,	Nice hat. He won't need it either.
The right of sepulchers, were shorn away	
To live a second life on second head,	Nice belt. He won't need this.
GRAVEDIGGER ONE:	
Ere beauty's dead fleece made another gay.	Nice boots. They are just my size.
GRAVEDIGGER TWO:	
In him those holy hours are seen,	
Without all ornament, itself and true,	Nice watch. Very expensive.
GRAVEDIGGER ONE:	
Making no summer of another's green,	I want that watch.

GRAVEDIGGER TWO:
Robbing no old to dress his beauty new;

No, I want it.

GRAVEDIGGER ONE:
And him as for a map doth Nature store,

Well, I'll have to fight you for it.

To show false Art what beauty was of yore.

"Dead" body awakens, sits up, grabs his watch back as Gravediggers, horrified, run off. "Dead" body now passes out again with a smile on his face. The gravediggers can use a flask instead of the watch. In which case at the end the "dead" body arises, snatches back his flask, takes a drink, and passes out again.)

SHAKESPEARE SONNETS AS SCENES

SONNET 69
"Those parts of thee that the world's eye doth view"

Cast: Young Man, Young Girl, Mother, Artist

Paired with Sonnets 3 and 62   1) Sonnet 69   2) Sonnet 3   3) Sonnet 62

1) Sonnet 69 is Young Girl trying to get the attention of the Young Man. 2) Sonnet 3 is the Young Man's Mother trying to get him to pay attention to the Young Girl. 3) Sonnet 62 begins after an Artist has offered to draw a picture of the Young Man. At the end of Sonnet 62 the artist shows a picture of a horse's ass. Mother and Young Girl find this hilarious.

YOUNG GIRL: SUBTEXT

Those parts of thee that the world's eye doth view
Want nothing that the thought of hearts can mend;
All tongues, the voice of souls give thee that due,
Utt'ring bare truth, even so as foes commend.

(Young Girl flattering Young Man to make him like her.)

Thy outward thus with outward praise is crowned,	Wait a minute.
But those same tongues that give thee so thine own	He's not paying attention to me.
In other accents do this praise confound	I don't understand.
By seeing farther than the eye hath shown.	Does he need glasses?
They look into the beauty of thy mind,	
And that in guess they measure by thy deeds;	
Then, churls, their thoughts, although their eyes were kind	Well, I never! You are vain and conceited.
To thy fair flower add the rank smell of weeds;	
But why thy odor matcheth not they show,	You are rotten!
The soil is this, that thou dost common grow.	Forget it!

(Young Girl exits.)

If Mini Play: Young Girl goes back to the Mother and shrugs as if to say, "I tried."

98

SONNETS WITH SUBTEXT

SONNET 74
"But be contented. When that fell arrest"

Cast: Ensemble

Can be used as a Finale or Curtain Call. If more than six, the actors can double up on lines. Think of this as a thank you to the audience. The actors can interpret the lines how they choose to accomplish this.

Emphasis on thee, thou, thine, refers to the audience.

ACTOR ONE: SUBTEXT

But be contented. When that fell arrest
Without all bail shall carry me (*us*) away,

ACTOR TWO:
My (*our*) life hath in this line some interest
Which for memorial still with thee shall stay.

ACTOR THREE:
When thou reviewest this, thou dost review
The very part was consecrate to thee.

ACTOR FOUR:
The earth can have but earth, which is his due;
My (*our*) spirit is thine, the better part of me (*we*.)

ACTOR FIVE:
So then thou hast but lost the dregs of life,
The prey of worms, my (*our*) body being dear;

ACTOR SIX:
The coward conquest of a wretch's knife,
Too base of thee to be remembered.   *Make remembered rhyme*
                                                                           with dear – Remembreer.

ENSEMBLE (ALL):
The worth of that is that which it contains,
And that is this, and this with thee remains.

SHAKESPEARE SONNETS AS SCENES

SONNET 75
"So are you to my thoughts as food to life"

Cast: One or Two Actors

One Actor: Actor is sitting on a bench with a closed box on his/her lap. Contents of box is unknown, but is in fact fast food possibly a piece of pizza, French fries, a turkey leg, or whatever the actor may choose.

Two Actors: Actor One is eating pizza or turkey leg, or whatever the actor chooses. Actor Two is talking to Actor One who thinks Actor Two is talking about him/her when in fact Actor Two is talking about the food.

ACTOR TWO:	SUBTEXT
(Directs focus to contents in box.)	
So are you to my thoughts as food to life,	
Or as sweet-seasoned showers are to the ground;	
And for the peace of your I hold such strife	For what is inside the box, I won't let anyone have but me.
As 'twixt a miser and his wealth is found;	
(Show closed box to audience.)	
Now proud as an enjoyer, and anon	
Doubting the filching age will steal his treasure;	I'm scared someone might steal you!
Now counting best to be with you alone,	So I keep you private.
Then bettered that the world may see my pleasure;	Maybe I should share you?
Sometime all full with feasting on your sight,	I love just looking at you.
And by and by clean starv-ed for a look;	Maybe I'll just take a peek.
Possessing or pursuing no delight	Because you are the only thing that give me so much pleasure.
Save what is had or must from you be took.	
Thus do I pine and surfeit day by day,	I am famished for you and I will indulge that pleasure by eating you right now!
Or gluttoning on all, or all away.	

One Actor: Actor opens the box and reveals the food to audience.

Two Actors: Actor Two leans in to Actor One Actor One thinks Actor Two is going to kiss them, when Actor Two steals the food and walks off to Actor One's bewilderment.

SHAKESPEARE SONNETS AS SCENES

SONNET 109
"O, never say that I was false of heart"

Cast: Owner with dying dog named Rose

Actor can use a stuffed animal dog or a real dog if trained to lie still.

OWNER:	SUBTEXT
(Owner gently brushes dog on his/her lap.)	
O, never say that I was false of heart,	I wasn't always there.
Though absence seemed my flame to qualify.	
As easy might I from myself depart	I would change places with you in a second.
As from my soul, which in thy breast doth lie.	You are my soulmate in this life.
(Owner covers dog with blanket to keep her warm.)	
That is my home of love; if I have ranged,	
Like him that travels, I return again,	I always come home to you.
Just to the time, not with the time exchanged,	I am sorry if I wasn't there enough.
So, that myself bring water for my stain.	It is my fault that you were alone.
(Owner hugs dog gently.)	
Never believe, though in my nature reigned	But never doubt, regardless of all of that…
All frailties that besiege all kinds of blood,	
That it could so preposterously be stained	You could never be anything but the best dog a person could ever have.
To leave for nothing all thy sum of good;	
(Dog dies.)	
For nothing this wide universe I call	In all the world, my Rose, you are my world.
Save thou, my Rose; in it thou art my all.	The best of the best.

SONNETS WITH SUBTEXT

SONNET 116
"Let me not to the marriage of true minds"

Cast: Young Girl, her husband-to-be, her father, the preacher, wedding guests, one in particular known as Wedding Guest One.

Paired with Sonnet 14: The witches from Macbeth exited having just recited Sonnet 14.

PREACHER:
Dearly beloved, if anyone here has just cause why these two young people should not be wed, speak now or forever hold your peace.

WEDDING GUEST ONE:

(Stands to give his blessing to the couple.)

Let me not to the marriage of true minds
Admit impediments; love is not love
Which alters when it alteration finds,
Or bends with the remover to remove.

(Satisfied with himself he sits to the confusion of the other wedding guests.)

PREACHER:
Thank you.
Now, if anyone here has just cause why these two young people should not be wed, speak now…

WEDDING GUEST ONE:

(He jumps up, having more to say.)

O, no, it is an ever-fix-ed mark
That looks on tempests and is never shaken;
It is the star to every wand'ring bark,
Whose worth's unknown, although his height be taken.

(Again, very satisfied with himself he sits.)

PREACHER:

(Trying to hurry up before he gets interrupted again.)
Speak now or forever hold – your -

WEDDING GUEST ONE:

(Stands one more time. By this time the other guests are getting irritated with him. But he goes on, seeing himself as love's expert.)
Love's not Time's fool, though rosy lips and cheeks
Within his bending sickle's compass come;
Love alters not with his brief hours and weeks,
But bears it out even to the edge of doom.

(At this point we hear a cry out from the bride-to-be. We now see she is with child and going into labor. The father and groom quickly help her out as the Preacher yells.)

PREACHER:
Say "I do!" Say "I do!"

BRIDE: *(yells)*
I do!

GROOM: *(yells)*
I do!

PREACHER: *(running after them)*
I now pronounce you husband and wife!

(Off stage we hear the cry of a new born baby. With a collective sigh of relief the wedding guests applaud.)

WEDDING GUEST:
If this be error and upon me proved,
I never writ, nor no man ever loved.

SONNETS WITH SUBTEXT

SONNET 120
"That you were once unkind befriends me now"

Cast: Lady Fair, Third Suitor (from Sonnet 18)

Paired back-to-back with Sonnets 18, 141/147 1) Sonnet 18 2) Sonnets 141 and 147 3) Sonnet 120. As the two rejected suitors from Sonnet 18, having shown their disappointment and despair in Sonnets 141 and 147 sink down, Lady Fair and Third Suitor return, apparently having a lover's spat. Both Suitors One and Two listen intently wanting the couple to break up, cheering on Lady Fairl until Lady Fair and Third Suitor make up. Realizing all hope is lost Suitors One and Two retreat to the nearest pub to drown their sorrows in a pint of ale.

LADY FAIR:	SUBTEXT
That you were once unkind befriends me now	How could you be so cruel.
And for that sorrow which I then did feel	And not care that you hurt me.
SUITOR THREE:	
Need must I under my transgression bow,	You are taking this too hard.
Unless my nerves were brass or hammered steel.	You try my patience.
LADY FAIR:	
For if you were by my unkindness shaken,	If you felt as I do you would know how hurt I am.
As I by yours, y'have passed a hell of time,	
SUITOR THREE:	
And I, a tyrant, have no leisure taken	Oh, I'm such a monster that I don't have feelings?
To weigh how once I suffered in your crime.	Really?
LADY FAIR:	
O, that our night of woe might have rememb'red	Oh, how I wish our wonderful night was not ruined.
My deepest sense how hard true sorrow hits,	How sad. I still love you.

SUITOR THREE:
And soon to you, as you to me then, tend'red
The humble salve which wounded bosoms fits!
But that your trespass now becomes a fee;

LADY FAIR:
Mine ransoms yours, and yours must ransom me.

I also wish it had never ended.
And I love you still!
Oh, I forgive all, my love.

And I too, am still in love with you!

If a Mini-Play: The couple kiss passionately and head off, presumably to be alone for their lovemaking. The rejected suitors walk off together in the opposite direction, presumably to a pub to drink their sorrows away.

SONNETS WITH SUBTEXT

SONNET 128
"How oft, when thou, my music, music play'st"

Cast: Musician, Musician's Biggest Fan, Two or Three Groupies

A Musician has just finished his song. (the musician could actually play an entire song, the end of a song, or a final chord to the song. He is surrounded by adoring fans, "Groupies." Song concludes; he puts his instrument on the chair, and rises to greet his fans. They exit with him signing their programs. His Biggest Fan is left on stage, sees the instrument, and starts to call after him, but it's too late. The fan, talking about her love for the musician, directs the sonnet to his instrument.

BIGGEST FAN:
(Looks lovingly at the instrument.)
How oft, when thou, my music, music play'st
Upon that blessed wood whose motion sounds

(She approaches the instrument.)
With thy sweet fingers when thou gently sway'st
The wiry concord that mine ear confounds,

(She touches the instrument.)
Do I envy those jacks that nimble leap
To kiss the tender inward of thy hand,

(She picks up the instrument.)
Whilst my poor lips, which should that harvest reap,
At the wood's boldness by thee blushing stand.

(She walks around with the instrument.)
To be so tickled, they would change their state
And situation with those dancing chips
O'er whom thy fingers walk with gentle gait,

(She puts it back on the chair.)
Making dead wood more blest than living lips.

Since saucy jacks so happy are in this,

(She gently kisses the instrument.)

Give them thy fingers, me thy lips to kiss.

Musician and groupies return. Musician picks up his instrument and again leaves with the groupies without noticing the Biggest Fan.

SONNET 130
"My mistress' eyes are nothing like the sun"

Cast: Man

Man complimenting his Lady Love in a rather awkward fashion. Another version could be an owner talking about their dog.

MAN
My mistress' eyes are nothing like the sun;
Coral is far more red than her lips' red;
If snow be white, why then her breasts are dun;
If hairs be wires, black wires grow on her head.

I have seen roses damasked, red and white;
But no such roses see I in her cheeks,
And in some perfumes is there more delight
Than in the breath that from my mistress reeks.

I love to hear her speak, yet well I know
That music hath a far more pleasing sound.
I grant I never saw a goddess go;
My mistress when she walks treads on the ground.

And yet, by heaven, I think my love as rare
As any she belied with false compare.

SONNET 138
"When my love swears that she is made of truth"

Cast: Older Rich Lady (cougar)

Older rich lady talking about her young lover. If her lover is a man, change the "she" to "he." There is no need for subtext as it is very clear what she is talking about.

OLDER RICH LADY (COUGAR):
When my love swears that she is made of truth,
I do believe her though I know she lies,
That she might think me some untutored youth,
Unlearned in the world's false subtleties.

Thus vainly thinking that she thinks me young,
Although she knows my days are past the best,
Simply I credit her false-speaking tongue;
On both sides thus is simple truth suppressed.

But wherefore says she not she is unjust?
And wherefore say not I that I am old?
O, love's best habit is in seeming trust,
And age in love loves not to have years told.

Therefore I lie with her, and she with me,
And in our faults by lies we flattered be.

SONNETS WITH SUBTEXT

SONNET 139
"O, call not me to justify the wrong"

Cast: SOLDIER

DYING SOLDIER: SUBTEXT
(Dying on battlefield, to his trusty sword.)

O, call not me to justify the wrong	I ache. Don't ask me to defend what we did in battle.
That thy unkindness lays upon my heart; Wound me not with thine eye but with thy tongue;	Your battle sound cannot hurt me.
Use power with power and slay me not by art.	With your blade at my side I can die.
Tell me thou lov'st elsewhere; but in my sight, Dear heart, forbear to glance thine eye aside;	Your blade has killed many. You do not have to face what you have done.
What need'st thou wound with cunning when thy might	Oh, why lay here when I can kill myself with you.
Is more than my o'erpressed defense can bide?	I am overpowered by weakness.
Let me excuse thee; ah, my love well knows	I'll forgive you, my trusty companion,
Her pretty looks have been mine enemies,	though your reputation has caused my enemies to seek me out.
And therefore from my face she turns my foes,	Together we have slain so many foes.
That they elsewhere might dart their injuries.	They know to stay away from us.
Yet do not so; but since I am near slain,	If one of them could only come back and finish me off.
Kill me outright with looks and rid my pain.	Or I could do it myself with you.

(Soldier dies.)

111

SONNET 141
"In faith I do not love thee with mine eyes"

Cast: Lover

As a Stand Alone: no subtext needed; it speaks for itself.

Paired with Sonnet 147. Two jilted lovers of the same woman trade quatrains, with their sorrows.

LOVER
In faith I do not love thee with thine eyes,
For they in thee a thousand errors note;
But 'tis my heart that loves what they despise,
Who in despite of view is pleased to dote.

Nor are mine ears with thy tongue's tune delighted,
Nor tender feeling to base touches prone,
Nor taste, nor smell, desire to be invited
To any sensual feast with thee alone.

But my five wits nor my five senses can
Dissuade one foolish heart from serving thee,
Who leaves unswayed the likeness of a man,
Thy proud heart's slave and vassal wretch to be.

Only my plague thus far I count my gain,
That she that makes me sin awards me pain.

SONNETS WITH SUBTEXT

SONNETS 141/147
"In faith I do not love thee with mine eyes"
"My love is as a fever, longing still"

Cast: Two Suitors

Two Jilted Lovers for the same woman lamenting their loss. As sonnet progresses each trying to out "grieve" the other. These are known as Suitor One and Suitor Two in Sonnet 18.

Jilted Lover One is very angry about this whereas Jilted Lover Two is very sad.

Paired with Sonnets 18 and 120.   1) Sonnet 18   2) Sonnets 141/147   3) Sonnet 120

<u>JILTED LOVER ONE: (SUITOR ONE)</u>
(To girl who has just left with Suitor Three.)
In faith I do not love thee with mine eyes,
For they in thee a thousand errors note;
But 'tis my heart that loves what they despise,
Who in despite of view is pleased to dote.

(Also, to girl who has just left with Suitor Three.)
<u>JILTED LOVER TWO: (SUITOR TWO)</u>
My love is as a fever, longing still
For that which longer nurseth the disease,
Feeding on that which doth preserve the ill,

(Tries to top his rival.)
<u>JILTED LOVER ONE: (SUITOR ONE)</u>
Nor are mine ears with thy tongue's tune delighted,
Nor tender feeling to base touches prone,
Nor taste, nor smell, desire to be invited
To any sensual feast with thee alone.

(Tries to top his rival.)
<u>JILTED LOVER TWO: (SUITOR TWO)</u>
The reason, my physician to my love,

Angry that his prescriptions are not kept,
Hath left me, and I desperate now approve
Desire is death, which physic did except.

(Now it has become a back and forth – who can top the other.)
JILTED LOVER ONE: (SUITOR ONE)
But my five wits nor my five senses can
Dissuade one foolish heart from serving thee,
Thy proud heart's slave and vassal wretch to be.

(The bout continues.)
JILTED LOVER TWO: (SUITOR TWO)
Past cure I am, now reason is past care,
And frantic-mad with evermore unrest;
My thoughts and my discourse as madmen's are,
At random from the truth vainly express:

(The bout heightens.)
JILTED LOVER ONE: (SUITOR ONE)
Only my plague thus far I count my gain,

JILTED LOVER TWO: (SUITOR TWO)
For I have sworn thee fair, and thought thee bright,

JILTED LOVER ONE: (SUITOR ONE)
That she that makes me sin awards me pain.

JILTED LOVER TWO: (SUITOR TWO)
Who art as black as hell, as dark as night.

SONNETS WITH SUBTEXT

SONNET 144
"Two loves I have, of comfort and despair"

Cast: Guy, Girl, Devil, Angel

A girl enters walking across the stage, and unbeknownst to her, drops her wallet. Along comes a guy walking across the stage, spots the wallet, and picks it up, putting it in his pocket. Back comes the girl looking for the wallet and asks if he has seen it. He shakes his head "no." She goes to edge of stage quietly crying. Enter his "conscience" depicted by an angel and a devil.

<u>GUY:</u>
(He looks her way and is torn between giving the wallet back to her or keeping it.)

Two loves I have of comfort and despair,

(He acknowledges the presence of his angel and devil.)

Which like two spirits do suggest me still;
The better angel is a man right fair,
The worser spirit a woman colored ill.

(Devil gestures for him to keep the wallet.)

To win me soon to hell, my female evil
Tempteth my better angel from my side,
Wooing his purity with her foul pride.

(Angel motions for him to give it back. Meanwhile Devil is trying to seduce the angel.)

And whether that my angel be turned fiend
Suspect I may, yet not directly tell;
But being both from me, both to each a friend,
I guess one angel is another's hell.

(He stops them. He has made his decision.)

Yet this shall I ne'er know, but live in doubt,
Til my bad angel fire my good one out.

If the actor chooses to let his angel win, he give the girl back her wallet then exits with his happy angel and his unhappy devil. If not, he keeps the wallet and exits with his happy devil and his unhappy angel.

115

SHAKESPEARE SONNETS AS SCENES

SONNET 145
"Those lips that Love's own hand did make"

Cast: Mother, Daughter

This sonnet is written in tetrameter (four iambic "feet"), instead of pentameter (five iambic "feet.") The emphasis on the syllables is now four (not five) short-long, short-long, short-long, short-long.

MOTHER:
(Have mother and daughter had an argument?)
Those lips that Love's own hand did make
Breathed forth the sound that said,

(Spoken, not directly to Mother.)
DAUGHTER:
"I hate."

MOTHER:
To me that languished for her sake.
But when she saw my woeful state,

Straight in her heart did mercy come,
Chiding that tongue that ever sweet
Was used in giving gently doom,
And taught it thus anew to greet:

DAUGHTER:
"I hate,"

MOTHER:
She altered with an end
That followed it as gentle day
Doth follow night, who, like a fiend,
From heaven to hell is flown away.

DAUGHTER:
"I hate:

MOTHER:
From hate away she threw,
And saved my life, saying,

DAUGHTER:
"not you."

The argument is over and the pair are at peace with each other. Daughter turns to Mother and they hug.

SHAKESPEARE SONNETS AS SCENES

SONNET 148
"O me, what eyes hath Love put in my head"

Cast: Guy with glasses and his Girlfriend

Paired with Sonnet 50: special script with both sonnets.

GUY: SUBTEXT

(Girlfriend has taken his glasses and is teasing him to come and get them. He is trying but finding it difficult, as he is practically blind without them.)

O me, what eyes hath Love put in my head
Which have no correspondence with true sight!
Or, if they have, where is my judgment fled,
That censures falsely what they see aright?

(Girlfriend sneaks up behind him, offers him the glasses and then snatches them away again.)

It that be fair whereon my false eyes dote,
What means the world to say it is not so?
If it be not, then love doth well denote
Love's eye is not so true as all men's no.   How can she do this to me?
                                                   This isn't funny.

(The teasing continues.)
How can it be? O, how can Love's eye be true,
That is so vexed with watching and with tears?
No marvel then though I mistake my view;   Maybe she's not so good a
                                                   girlfriend.
The sun itself sees not till heaven clears.   I see than now.

O cunning Love, with tears though keep'st   But I still love her.
me blind,
(Girlfriend gives him back his glasses and a loving kiss on the cheek.)
Lest eyes well-seeing thy foul faults should find.

(Happy now, the Guy takes his Girlfriend in his arms and gives her a good kiss on the lips.)

Glossary with Sonnets Listed in Numerical Order

The following vocabulary list is offered as a tool to determine what the words meant in the original poems. The actor can then decide, when creating their sonnets as scenes, if they want to use this definition, or make up one of their own.

First, here are a few often used Elizabethan words and their contemporary meanings:

WORD	MEANING	WORD	MEANING
Anon	soon	Privy	inform, share
Dost	do	Thee/Thou	you
Doth	does	Thy	your
Ere	before	Tidings	news
Hie	go quickly	Wherefore	why
Pray	beg	Whereto	to which

SHAKESPEARE SONNETS AS SCENES

SONNET	WORD	POSSIBLE MEANING
3	repair	make ready
	beguile	deceive
	unbless	to deprive of a blessing
	uneared	virgin
	disdains	removes
	tillage	cultivated land
	husbandry	to manage carefully
	posterity	future, offspring
14	dearths	insufficient amounts
	convert	to alter, make different
	prognosticate	make a prediction
	quality	nature, character
18	temperate	mild, moderate
	ow'st	have, own, possess
	brag	prideful, spirited
19	devouring	to consume greedily
	blunt	dull, insensitive
	brood	to hatch, to conceive
	keen	sharp
	heinous	hateful, wicked
	untainted	pure, free of contamination
26	vassalage	service, subordination
	embassage	message
	wit	ability to use words in a clever and humorous way

GLOSSARY WITH SONNETS LISTED IN NUMERICAL ORDER

SONNET	WORD	POSSIBLE MEANING
	conceit	estimation or opinion of something
	aspect	a way in which something can be viewed by the mind
	apparel	clothing
	tottered	unstable
29	beweep	cry, weep
	scope	opportunities
33	sovereign	supreme authority
	gilding	process of applying gold glint to a surface
	alchemy	seemingly magical power
	visage	journey
33	region	a large segment of space
	whit	least bit
	distaineth	stain the honor of
41	befits	suits
	forbear	delay
	chide	scold
43	unrespected	unnoticed, unobserved
50	repose	sleep, rest
	measured	calculated, determined
53	substance	matter, that which has mass and occupies space
	whereof	of what
	tend	attend
	Adonis	beautiful, sexually attractive man
	counterfeit	imitation

121

SHAKESPEARE SONNETS AS SCENES

SONNET	WORD	POSSIBLE MEANING
	Helen	most beautiful woman
	tires	clothing
	foison	harvest, abundance
	bounty	reward, payment
	constant	steadfast, unchanging
57	chide	scold
62	surmount	overcome, top
	tanned	finished
	Antiquity	age, being old
	contrary	opposite
	iniquity	a grossly immoral act
66	desert	barren area of landscape
	jollity	merriment, celebration
	forsworn	lied
66	gilded	having the color or quality of gold
	strumpeted	prostituted
	folly	costly or ruinous outcome
68	bastard	unfortunate
	durst	persuaded to
	tresses	long lock of hair
	sepulchers	tombs, burial vaults
	fleece	coat of wool
	ornament	something that decorates or adorns
69	commend	praise
	accents	pronunciation

GLOSSARY WITH SONNETS LISTED IN NUMERICAL ORDER

SONNET	WORD	POSSIBLE MEANING
	confound	make worse
	measure	achieve
	churls	rude people
	rank	grade
	show	display
	common	frequently
74	fell	fierce, cruel
	arrest	authority
	bail	security, money
	consecrate	declared
	dregs	least desirable
	base	of little value
75	enjoyer	a person who delights in having an experience
	filching	stealing
	pine	wither away, mourn
	surfeit	overindulge, feed to excess
	gluttoning	eating to excess
109	false	untrue
	flame	intense passion
	qualify	modify, restrict
	ranged	wandered
	besiege	surround, crowd in
	preposterously	absurdly, unreasonably
	sum	whole amount

123

SHAKESPEARE SONNETS AS SCENES

SONNET	WORD	POSSIBLE MEANING
116	impediments	hindrances, defects
	alteration	change
	tempests	violent storm
	bark	harsh sound (uttered by a dog)
	height	highest point
	sickle's	reaper, cutting instrument
120	transgression	breach, violation of duty
	tend'red	offered
	salve	flattery
	trespass	intrusion, breach
128	wiry	lean, sinewy
	concord	harmony
	confounds	frustrates, perplexes
	saucy	playful, lively
	damask'd	in silk cloth
130	dun	dull, grayish brown
	belied	misrepresented, contradicted
138	subtleties	caginess, craftiness
	unjust	unfair, dishonest
139	o'er pressed	crushed, overwhelmed
	bide	wait for
139	dart	direct
141	vassal	subordinate, slave
144	suggest	proposing, say indirectly

GLOSSARY WITH SONNETS LISTED IN NUMERICAL ORDER

SONNET	WORD	POSSIBLE MEANING
145	languished	pined away
	woeful	mournful, unhappy
	chiding	scolding
	doom	ruin, judgment
147	physic	drug
	discourse	speaking
	bright	full of light
148	correspondence	agreement
	censures	judges
	dote	show fondness, love
	vexed	distressed
	marvel	wonder
	cunning	delicately pleasing; pretty or cute

Acknowledgments

My complete and heartfelt thank you to all below who in one way or another greatly and lovingly contributed to the final manuscript and the workshops that resulted from it.

Kelsey and Caroline Lenz

Lèna Chillingerian, Lewis and Carol Coe, Dr. Christina R. Hathaway, Sharon Okenquist, Scott Nelson, Ryan Schaefer, Father John Spino, John Briggs, editor, Asya Blue, book designer, Dawn Frederick, proofreader

Union County Vo/Tech High School Performing Arts Academy, Scotch Plains NJ, Kathleen Aiellos, Heather Lessing

The Original 2019 New York Renaissance Faire Sonneteers
Zak Barnett
Lee Ann Brown
Carter Glace
Ann Glachin
Joe Hughes
Cordelia Lucid
Karina Brunori Lucid
Francis Mabborang
Charley Marlowe

Tina M. Nostro
Lorraine Ruth Rosenberg

Grace Ahlin, Matthew Duncan, Julie Gaarskjaer,
Julia Rebecca Gross, Tyler Miranda,

Adam O'Connell, Christina Polichetti, Jason Radcliffe,
Jesse Rosien, Griffin Wood

My sincere apologies to any and all I may have
inadvertently missed. Thank you.